Dartmouth Out Of Doors: A Book Descriptive Of The Outdoor Life In And About Hanover, New Hampshire

Fred Henry Harris

DARTMOUTH
OUT. O' DOORS

**A Book Descriptive of the Outdoor Life
in and about Hanover, N. H.**

Compiled and Edited for the

Outing Club by

FRED H. HARRIS, '11

PRINT OF
GEORGE E. CROSBY COMPANY
BOSTON, MASS.
1913

Ski-Jumping at Hanover.   Drawn for the Outing Club by W. B. Humphrey, '14

Table of Contents

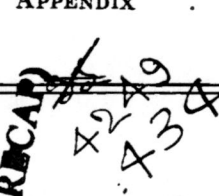

Dartmouth College

1,300 STUDENTS   ## Hanover, N. H.   **108 INSTRUCTORS**

LOCATION   The College is situated on an upland terrace above the Connecticut River in the high hill-country of middle New Hampshire and Vermont.

HISTORY   Founded by royal charter from George III, December 18th, 1769. The charter of the college was an outgrowth of a plan of the Reverend Eleazer Wheelock for the education of Indians which had its first development in the foundation in 1754 of Moor's Indian Charity School at Lebanon, Conn. In 1816 the State of New Hampshire attempted to gain control of the college. The case was fought through the lower courts and finally carried to the Supreme Court of the United States. Mr. Webster in an argument of great eloquence and power presented the case of his Alma Mater. Decision favorable to the college was rendered by Chief Justice Marshall in 1819. This decision in the now famous "Dartmouth College Case" was cast in such broad terms that it has been characterized as "in its effects more far-reaching and of more general interest than perhaps any other decision ever made in this country."

The courses of undergraduate instruction offered by the college lead to the degrees of Bachelor of Arts and Bachelor of Science.

The Associated Graduate Schools:

The Amos Tuck School of Administration and Finance   A school offering two years of special preparation for business careers. Students of three years' undergraduate standing admitted to the work of the first year which leads to the bachelor's degree.

The work of this year lays a foundation for the specialized work of the second year. Students with the bachelor's degree are admitted to the work of the second year, which leads to the degree of Master of Commercial Science.

—H. S. PERSON, *Director.*

The Thayer School of Civil Engineering   Established 1871, offers a general course of study and practice in Civil Engineering, so developed as to include the essential principles of all important branches through two years of professional preparation.

—ROBERT FLETCHER, *Director.*

The Medical School   Established 1797. The course covers four years of lectures, laboratory and recitation work, with clinics and ward classes at the Mary Hitchcock Memorial Hospital. This hospital, widely known as one of the best cottage hospitals in the country, is under the management of physicians and surgeons who are connected with the Medical School.—J. M. GILE, M.D., *Dean.*

Application for admission to the college should be addressed to Craven Laycock, Dean: for admission to the Associated Graduate Schools to the appropriate Director or Dean of the school to which admission is sought: other correspondence to W. Gray Knapp, Secretary.

Dartmouth College
Hanover, N. H.

Introduction

THE purpose of this book is fourfold. First, it aims to show the possibilities of winter outing by means of stories of actual trips taken by Dartmouth students to points of interest easily accessible from Hanover. A good many of these stories, if we, for the moment, ignore the familiarity of New England names, might well seem to have their setting in Switzerland rather than in New Hampshire. They have all the zest and interest that is usually expected only of reminiscences of the Alps or the Tyrol.

It is a fair assumption that he who reads these experiences will be seized with a desire to try the thing for himself. He may not care to venture far at first. Skis and snowshoes may be more or less unknown quantities; muscles may not be trained for the long hike, but here are provided data concerning a long series of trails leading from the campus; short ones for the beginner, long ones for the practised tramper. Having, then, first provided the incentive, this book, secondly, points the way.

For the benefit, further, of the less experienced, considerable space is devoted to a consideration of the apparatus of outing. In summer time we can get along fairly well with any ill assorted equipment. In winter the case is quite different. What to take and how to use what is taken may be matters of vital importance. Chapters are, accordingly, devoted not only to the "why" and the "where" of outing, but to the "how" as well. That very nearly covers the case.

A book of this kind, emanating from Dartmouth,

would not be complete, however, without considerable mention of the organization which has opened the eyes of Dartmouth men to the real joys of Hanover winters: —the Outing Club. Except for the activities of this organization, *Dartmouth Out O' Doors* would never have been compiled. That the fourth purpose of the book should be to commemorate the Dartmouth Outing Club, to outline its history and to bespeak the interest of all red-blooded persons in furthering its work, is certainly fitting.

A first attempt of this kind is necessarily imperfect. It is realized that many faults in selection and arrangement will be immediately obvious even to the casual reader. It is, however, the hope that the book will arouse sufficient interest to justify occasional new editions until the highest standard of accuracy and completeness has been achieved. Additions, corrections and helpful suggestions will be most gratefully received.

HOMER EATON KEYES.

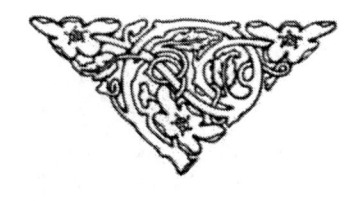

Acknowledgment

A FEELING of hearty co-operation and practical help has been the keynote of the work on this book from the start, and to the officers and friends of the Outing Club, with whose help the compilation of this book has alone been possible, the editor wishes to express his appreciation and sincere thanks.

Although the idea had been in mind for some time, it was not until President Nichols suggested the portrayal of this unique feature of Dartmouth life that the book began to take concrete form, and a pleasant feature of the work throughout has been the interest and encouragement with which Dr. Nichols has lent the project his support.

To Professors E. F. Clark, G. F. Hull, J. W. Goldthwaite and A. H. Licklider, I wish to express many thanks not only for their help in connection with this book but for their support in the organizing of the Club itself, for from the very first, the Outing Club has counted them among its mainstays.

For going over the book and giving helpful criticisms and suggestions, acknowledgment is due Professor C. D. Adams and A. H. Licklider. For help in arrangement, revisions, and in writing the introduction of this book, I acknowledge inestimable assistance from Professor H. E. Keyes.

For illustrations, the book is largely indebted to D. E. Adams, '13, for his pictures of the White Mountains. Other contributors are W. Lee White, '12, F. H. Harris, '11, Mr. Rugg, Professor Goodrich,

Ray W. Tobey, '12, C. E. Shumway, '13 and F. A. Seidler, '13. The frontispiece and the smaller comic sketches were drawn by W. B. Humphrey, '14.

Without reference to the present officers of the Club, C. E. Shumway, M. C. Avery, J. Y. Cheney and D. E. Adams, this acknowledgment would be far from complete; for true co-operation, contributions and help cheerfully rendered, I express to them my grateful appreciation.   F. H. H.

A Salute of the Trail
By W. Lee White, '12

EACH successive generation is called upon to weigh judicially its allotted quota of new enterprises and the *prophet without honor in his own country* was favored indeed in comparison with the average promoter of new college activities. The blasts of ridicule and chaff, of censoriousness

The Lone Ski-runner

and skepticism, that oppose the advance of any new addition to existing organizations, by contrast make the burdens of a suffragist leader seem light indeed. In the face of this always present reluctance to surrender the merest sliver of tradition, fortunate forsooth is the man who can carry through to a permanent place any new addition to the schedule of undergraduate life.

During the early weeks of the winter of 1909-10 a lone ski-runner wound to and fro of an afternoon from a home-made ski-jump on the quartz ledges back of Davison's farm. And as he dipped and rose from gully to gully he marvelled, that, with a thousand blooded men so near, he rarely saw a ski-track save his own, and traces of the webbed feet were all too few. And, sensing to the full the thrill of rapid travel and the lure of beaten snows waist deep, he vowed his uttermost endeavor in sounding through the lengths of listless corridors the call of the joyous winter to those who wait but for excuse and company to trade the blue of pipe smoke for the purple glint of frozen sunlight.

Then, in response to the call printed in *The Dartmouth* of January nine, nineteen hundred and ten, some fifty men, all eager to escape the tedium of winter behind bolts, drew up a pact to form an Outing Club, and chose the lone ski-runner, F. H. Harris, President and first leader of this venture. So well he led, that now, within the limits of three years, the Club has gained a solid seat in the councils of the college and its great gala day—The Winter Carnival—is settled as an institution, unique and symbolical of the Dartmouth winter. The great load, the burden of carrying through this self-suggested task, fell heavily and entirely upon its venturesome author. For two whole winters it was Fred who routed the lazy out into the drifts; kept *The Dartmouth* and the New England dailies supplied with Outing Club news; shouldered personally impeding financial difficulties; injected huge blocks of his enthusiasm into every wavering tyro, and of a week-end was always on hand in person to lead away from Dartmouth Hall. But now, from some near vantage point, he sees a *college* out on trails where two score months ago meagre and lonesome tracks were all that broke the surface of the hills.

To-day, from the ranks of the Alumni, he has rather gained than lost in his enthusiasm for our winter club. For his inexhaustible energy in bringing together and making possible this, our first Year Book; for his time spent in opening the opportunities of our great Hanover winter; for his untiring skill on the snow path; for his good comradeship on many a trip; for all this we are happy in once again giving him a salute of the frozen trail and urgently bidding him to our coming Carnival, lest the surge and slap of a familar ski be wanting when the bugle signals "All clear below!"

The Dartmouth Outing Club

ITS HISTORY, ITS PRESENT WORK AND ITS FUTURE AMBITIONS

"Daughter of the woods and hills, Dartmouth, my stern
Rock-boned and wind-brown sibyl of the snows."
Richard Hovey

IF you love the great out-of-doors, and if you like to live, really live, in the clean, wide, distant sweep of a limitless horizon, breathe an untainted air, boundless as the heavens themselves, and enjoy a freedom that can be found in no other way, a keen, stimulating, exhilarating pleasure that thrills you through the very center of your being, you will understand what motives led to the organization of the Dartmouth Outing Club. This unique organization, which has attracted the attention of all lovers of outdoor sport, was formed during the winter of 1909 and 1910 by those who hoped better to realize the possibilities of the New Hampshire wilderness, who felt that four years spent in college without enjoying a few real, big, blissful moments of the freedom of the granite hills were years not enjoyed to the fullest advantage. It was hoped that the Club could teach its members new secrets of the woods; that, through it, they could enjoy the tonic that Nature puts for them into the wind, the sky, the sunshine, the spices of the pine and hemlock odors and the ozone of the great out-of-doors.

It was true that for many years the jagged tracks of the snowshoe crossed and recrossed the hills about the old New Hampshire college, and here and there could be seen the smooth, parallel tracks of the ski, indenting the mantle of white; but not until the formation of the Outing Club was there any attempt to put the sports of skiing or snowshoeing on the "scientific management" basis, nor were the wide opportunities offered by the ideal location at all developed. Starting in a modest way with 60 members, the success of the Club grew by leaps and bounds, and the

A Week-End Trip Over the Snow

enthusiasm it aroused and the co-operation it received the very first season proved that it filled a long-felt want, and that the Dartmouth Outing Club had come to stay. Instead of the long winter months being bemoaned as the one bane of existence in Hanover, it is now with a tinge of regret that the snows of winter are seen slowly melting away.

WEEK END TRIPS OVER THE SNOW

A very successful winter meet proved that the Club had its place in Dartmouth sports.   But it is not in such things as a winter carnival that the real purpose of the Club is shown.   The cross-country trips to points of interest are the things, after all.   This shows true love of the sport for the sport's sake, and it is among the men who join these week-end trips that the Club will need to look for its real supporters.   It is on these long "hikes" over the snow-clad hills of Vermont and New Hampshire that there is felt the keen, stimulating, uncloying pleasure in being alive that thrills to the very bone sinew, and makes muscle, blood, strength and fire, and builds up bodies and repairs the waste of toil and worry.

SNOW CONDITIONS AT HANOVER IDEAL

Hanover lies in a snow belt which has for its southern boundary the southern part of the state, and whose northern boundary extends into Canada.   Below this belt, the humidity in the air seems to cause the snow storms to turn into rain, which leaves a crust (very inimical to good sport), and causes the snow soon to melt away.   Above this imaginary line, the snow-fall is not only heavier, but the air is drier and colder, which permits of the snow lying in the powdery, fluffy condition so necessary for good skiing or snow-shoeing.   This shows the reason why Dartmouth is so ideally located for winter sports.   Tucked away within an hour's travel from the campus are many interesting places.   Keeping straight on north, through the main street of the little near-by village of Norwich, for about a mile, you come to a barren knoll known as Meeting-house Hill; looking southward from here, down the

Connecticut river valley, you can see Mt. Ascutney looming up nineteen miles away. On the north, you can see Mt. Moosilauke, Smart's and Cube, and if the air be very clear, Mt. Lafayette can be discerned in the distance. If we can spare a little more time, we can go eastward eight miles to the Outing Club hut, and using that as a base of supplies, climb Moose Mountain, which towers above. By taking the train north to Thetford, and thence walking eastward six miles, we come to Holt's ledge, which on one side rolls away to the west and on the east presents a sheer, perpendicular drop of over 500 feet. From here we can obtain a closer view of Smart's and Cube, breaking the horizon only a few miles away.

If we follow up the Pompanoosuc River, which empties its waters into the Connecticut River five miles above Hanover, we come to "Campanoosuc," a comfortable abode, the use of which last winter was kindly offered members of the Outing Club. A few miles beyond are located the beautiful little mountain lakes, Lake Fairlee and Morey Lake. It will easily be seen how rich Dartmouth is in its surrounding spots of beauty. W. Lee White, president of the Outing Club for the season 1911-1912, aptly expresses the call of the out-doors in the following lines of his story, "Little Trips to Near-by Places":—

"It may at first thought seem scarce worth the trouble to try to sandwich a real out-of-doors trip into the narrow space between noon and night, but one experience will prove the contrary, and with knapsack ready packed by your desk-side, you can just as easily plan to stay out to supper. And when winter brings out the skis and snowshoes, there is an added delight in the creak and rattle of travel. If perchance you are a skeptic, beg, borrow or steal an old knapsack some afternoon, and slip off somewhere, where only the wood folk and the trees can see you, build your fire and boil your coffee. Then having stuffed full the old pipe, wander leisurely back to the campus after sundown, and see whether or not your brain is swept clean of the cobwebs of print and perhaps filled with quiet resolution to go back at some early date to that campfire and build it up again."

Through the Deep Woods

SKI AND SNOWSHOE

On these trips, much good-natured competition arises as to the relative merits of the snowshoe and the ski, among the followers of the same. It was aptly demonstrated at Hanover that a beginner on snowshoes can easily outdistance a novice on skis, because snowshoeing is so much easier to learn; but on the other hand the expert ski-runner can leave behind the best men on nowshoes, and the longer the trip, the more advantage there is noticed in favor of the ski. Although the snow-shoe has admittedly a field in which it is superior to the ski, such as thick underbrush on the side of a steep hill, yet it is also proved that all in all, up hill and down, over all kinds of country, the user of the ski can hold his own and a little more with the exponent of the webbed shoe, and have a good deal of sport besides.

AMBITIONS OF THE CLUB

A worthy ambition of the Club is to make from year to year a few lantern slides from the best negatives secured by its members on these trips. Over 100 slides have already been made, and in the course of time the Club promises to have an extremely valuable and interesting collection, illustrative of winter sports, and of New Hampshire scenery. These are thrown up in the form of a stereopticon lecture at the annual meetings and prove to be most interesting and instructive. Other good features are the card system and the information bureau introduced by Lee White, Secretary 1910-11. The card system keeps an exact account of what each member does in or for the Club, and the information bureau serves to enlighten members, alumni or guests as to the prospective trips, things to take and to wear, distances to certain mountains, and the like.

Another ambition of the Club, which is receiving the commendation of older and more experienced men in this line of work, such as John Ritchie, Jr., of the Appalachian Mountain Climbing Club, is to establish a chain of camps penetrating northward each year toward the White Mountains. It is even hoped that in time, connection will be established as far north as the Dartmouth grant, a tract of virgin wilderness, owned by the college, in the northern part of the state. The building of these cabins each year, especially as the distance from the base of supplies grows greater, necessitates the showing of a great deal of energy and determination, and success is only possible by securing great co-operation among the members of the Club and its friends. The route connecting these camps will lead over mountain ranges and through a wilderness little

A Hill Side in February

scarred by the signs of man. Whether he be fisherman, camper, or hunter, this "forest primeval," will present a paradise to the lover of the out-of-doors. This is the home of the speckled trout, the partridge, and the deer. Whether the followers of these trails be students off on a few days' vacation, made possible by careful husband-

Shadows

ing of their "cuts", or alumni revisiting the haunts of their youth, they cannot help catching the lure of the trail, feeling the added freshness and the sweet wild unrest in the air, which makes them years younger, and makes life seem sweeter than ever before.

A TYPICAL TOUR

Take a trip with us, if you will, to Moose Mountain. It is after a new fallen snow in February, and all the world is aglitter. As the blood begins to course through our veins, how much better we feel. The fetters are cast aside on the trail and man comes into his own. It is on a trip like this that we appreciate , the full meaning of those words of Robert Browning:

"God's in His Heaven,
All's right with the world."

How soft the snowshoe feels under foot, and what music is the swish, swish of the skis as they slip along. We have now reached the last mile of the trail which leads to where the Outing Club cabin nestles cozily in the heavy growth of evergreens and hardwoods at the base of the mountain. The trail is nearly obliterated; only a faint suggestion is left of the tracks of the party which passed this way two weeks before. As we proceed, Indian file, along the path through the deep woods, little cooling showers of snow send shivers down your back as you stoop beneath some heavily laden branch. A little clearing bursts upon you and the snow-shrouded form of a cabin is noticed on the other side. Ah! this is home indeed! It is with a sigh of contentment that we enter and cast off the knapsacks which have added pounds of weight since we started.

While one starts a fire in the big box stove, another goes to fill the pail with water from the little mountain brook which gurgles beside the cabin, and a third busies himself with cutting balsam boughs for the "bunks." A voice from the woods cries, "Say, this snow must be five feet deep here; gee! I'm in up to my waist; bring me my snow-shoes, or I will never be able to get these boughs out; will you, 'Shum'?" "Sure, if I ever get out of this myself," comes the answer. Soon the smoke is seen curling lazily from the chimney and things begin to look more like a camp. The chill begins to creep into the air and as the soft, black night comes down, and the shadows melt together through the lofty arches of the trees, and form a dusky, protecting curtain which rests your eyes and brain, it is with a sigh of contentment that you grasp your ax, shoulder your armful of firewood and creep to the cozy warmth of the cabin inside.

This cabin is above every other place the Mecca for the members of the Outing Club. The register kept in a tin can contains the record of many jolly week-end and over-night parties, and the fittings, equipment and even the planks of the cabin testify to the mechanical ingenuity and muscular strength of the Club members.

"Are you fellows hungry tonight?" says Lee, as the odor of frizzling bacon and frying beefsteak permeates the cabin. "Well, I guess I can take care of my share," Vic answers.

The simple, wholesome food from tin plates, the sparkling water from tin cups, are dainties fit for a king, and yet our life is more like that of the Indian. For a space, the silence is broken only by the sound of knives and forks, then "Cap" breaks forth with, "Say, do you suppose 'Eric' and 'Jack' and that bunch will try to get over after supper?" "They told me they would," says Lee, "I guess they'll make it." Then as the dishes are being washed, and the pipes lit up, the conversation becomes general. It is here that the day's sport is re-lived; the stories told, the plans made and friendship cemented.

By this time an honest weariness is creeping over us and we take a lingering look at the fir bed with its big double blankets. Can you imagine morphine or sleeping powders sneaking around such a couch to call sleep down to you?.

Nature has been generous to us with her tonic and we sleep, filling our lungs with the pure sweet air, crisp and cold, but yet a cold that warms and thickens the blood, rousing it from its sluggish action to new vigorous life. We are tired—but think of a day of toil in the city! Can the same definition be given to the word "tired" in the two cases? In the city we toss and worry; in the camp, we sleep and rest and wake up the next morning feeling wonderfully refreshed.

On these trips, the cabin becomes a palace, the open camp-fire your mirror in which you see your dream-life of freedom as it should be, wherein there is equality— brotherhood.

Truly, where is there a greater democracy than that of the great out-of-doors? Among all the lovers of winter sports there seems to be a kindred note, some basic principle. They meet on the same footing, the same spirit moves them all. It is the desire to get closer to Nature and really to live.

The following editorial, entitled "When Comfort becomes Confinement," by C. E. Snow, editor of *The Dartmouth,* strikes exceptionally well the keynote of the Outing Club:—

" Dartmouth students without snowshoes ought to be as rare as fish without fins. When the snow of the

Hanover winter flies thick and drifts deeply around house and hall, it is all very well to cry contentment in the glow of the open grate; the whistle of the radiator is music to ears that tingle. There arrives a time, however, when red blood threatens to grow stagnant, and comfort becomes confinement. When the sun shines brilliant on the snow, and blue sky and crystal air raise a longing that will not be found by rabbit-runs across the campus, then the long ski and the woven rawhide afford the only means of surmounting the imprisonment of a northern winter.

"The Outing Club might well be termed the 'organization for making the most of the Hanover winter.' Whether its members come trooping, on snowshoe and ski, ruddy-faced, from a trip to the hut at 'Campanoosuc,' or whether they return bronzed and bearded from piercing ice-clad trails above the White Mountain tree-line, they are to be envied by the pale and over-coated individual whose path leads from Morris chair to class room seat. Only those who have kindled a fire in the snow, and slept on balsam buds can tell adequately of the joys of the frozen trail.

"The winter sport is built for all manner of men. From the most hollow-chested plodder on snowshoes, to the strongest-limbed and surest-balanced rider of the ski, each emerges healthier and keener from every tumble in the snow. The cross-country tramp and the mountain climb are for the less strenuous participants; the dash, the run, and the ski-jump, for the winter athlete. The Outing Club is the crystallization of it all, and because it represents a group of sports that should be the most characteristic of Dartmouth activities, it should enroll the largest and most representative membership of any organization in college. Its rolls are open to the whole college and the whole college should enlist."

WINTER CARNIVAL AT HANOVER

Its second season found the Outing Club bigger and busier than ever, and, as the crowning event, there was held for the first time in the history of American colleges a Winter Carnival, which proved one of the most delightful events of the year. Many fair guests were

Cross-Country Snowshoe Racer Finishing

invited, and the occasion took on the magnitude of a junior "prom." Many of the alumni and others interested in winter sports took this opportunity to see Dartmouth at a time admittedly the most unique of the year. The meet started with preliminary ski and snowshoe dashes and the trials for the relay races on Faculty Pond. A great crowd assembled to see the cross-country ski and snowshoe runs, which started and finished at the Vale of Tempe. The cross-country snowshoe race offered a very close finish, "Wally" Jones winning first place, in 25 minutes, 29 and 3-5 seconds, with "Larry" Day but a few feet behind, and "Brutus" Holway a close third. The end of the cross-country ski race led down a steep hill and between two huge pine trees. As the first and second ski runners tore down the steep declivity at breakneck speed, scarcely a rod apart after four miles of strenuous effort, no more hair-raising finish could be desired. "Fred" Harris, '11, won first place in 24 minutes, $5\frac{1}{2}$ seconds, with "Ty" Cobb, '12, second and "Cap" Weston third.

Between the start and finish of the cross-country run, obstacle races were held, over brush fences, across gullies and up steep banks, and proved to be a "howling" success. In the evening, the college dramatic club presented "David Garrick" before a large and enthusiastic audience, and following this the first Outing Club dance was held at the Commons. The hall was attractively decorated with festoons of evergreen boughs, in keeping with the winter setting. Quite a contrast was apparent between the beautiful gowns worn at this festivity, and the "outing" costumes worn by the same women at the meet in the afternoon. Instead of moccasins, snowshoes, sweaters, and furs we saw low-neck gowns of shimmering silks and satin and high-heeled French pumps. During the intermission a bountiful repast was served in the grill. Altogether the first Outing Club dance was considered a great success.

Early Saturday afternoon, the final heats in the ski and snowshoe dashes were held, and the relay races pulled off. Following this came the hockey game, in which Capt. "Fred" Eaton led his team to a victory over the Massachusetts Agricultural College team.

Prize Winners — Winter Carnival

The scene then again shifted to the Vale of Tempe, where the ski-jumping contest was held. This proved to be the most interesting event of the day, illustrating the fact that American people are most interested in those sports where the element of chance runs high. A jumping platform had been built on a steep hill. The course was in ideal condition; although the snow had been sticky during the middle of the day, as the sun be-

One Hundred Yard Snowshoe Dash

came lower the air grew much colder and the surface hardened . The slide had been roped off, and when the contestants appeared a large crowd thronged the course.

The writer wishes to correct an erroneous impression quite prevalent among the American people, whose knowledge of ski-jumping is limited to pictures they have seen of jumpers in the air. The jump is made out and down and *never up*.

Starting far above, at a given signal, the jumper speeds with ever-increasing velocity toward the platform or "take-off." A scant few yards away, he crouches and as the brink is reached, hurls himself out erect and well balanced, into the space beyond. Then follows the hiss of the jumper's body, as it passes through the air, shooting out and down, landing lightly on the slope far below, then rushing out on the level plain beneath, to swerve suddenly, send up a cloud of snow, and end abruptly in a brilliantly executed "Telemark" swing.

A platform was built at the most advantageous point of the course, to the right and a little below the "take-off," to accommodate Mrs. Nichols, the wife of the President, and some twenty women of the faculty and their guests. The stand was attractively trimmed with hemlock and balsam boughs, and proved a most acceptable place from which to view the contest; in fact, a foot-hold on the steep slope at this point would otherwise have been impossible.

The program consisted of the "junior" and "novice" events on the small jump, and the "expert" event on the big jump. Much amusement was caused by the somersaults which some of the contestants took in the snow.

Little "Jack" Bowler, son of Dr. Bowler, the football trainer, won the junior event, while perhaps the best nerve was shown by the little 12-year-old "Dickie" Bowler, who negotiated the jump most successfully. W. H. Weston, Jr., won the novice jump. With these events run off, the interest turned to the senior event on the big jump. The places in this event were awarded according to a system of points, a certain number being added for form or gracefulness in the flight, and a certain

The Jumper Hurls Himself out into the Space Beyond

number being detracted for a fall.   To those spectators who had never seen any ski-jumping before, it seemed little short of marvelous, and the swift, downward flight, the spring, or "saats," as it is called in Norway, at the edge of the "take-off," followed by the swift rush through the air, and the graceful landing far down on the slope below, afforded a sight long to be remembered. Barely five points separated the first two men.   A. T. Cobb, '12, won first place, with 285 points, and F. H. Harris, '11, second with 280.

Perfect " Form" Shown by " Dickie" Bowler (Age 12)

SECOND WINTER CARNIVAL

In February, 1912, a second Winter Carnival was undertaken on a more pretentious scale than the first and proved to be an even greater success.

In general, the same plan was carried out as the year before.   The following resumé, in part from the college paper, may not be out of place:

"At three o'clock on Friday, when the hills had become thickly dotted with onlookers, the roll was called and the contestants prepared for the cross-country snowshoe race. As soon as the gun was fired, S. L. Day, '14, and A. S. Holway, '12, jumped into the lead and finished in the order named."

EXHIBITION SKI JUMP A NOVEL EVENT

"The spectators then mounted the hills and many visitors beheld ski-jumping for the first time. F. H.

Start of the Snowshoe Cross Country

Harris, '11, was back in his old form and his exhibition was much appreciated. The work of little twelve year old 'Dickie' Bowler on the big jump was the feature of the afternoon."

It was then announced that the cross-country ski race was to begin. The crowds had grown and now pressed around the contestants. A false start caused a comical mix-up and there was no little trouble in again lining up the contestants. A. T. Cobb, '12, took the lead at the start, plunging five yards ahead of Bache-Wiig, '15; J. Y. Cheney, '13, followed close.

OBSTACLE RACE AMUSES CROWDS

The Obstacle Race afforded an amusing part of the day's entertainment. While the men were preparing for the start down the Vale, a snowball fusillade broke loose from the students above, and the hill was straight-way attacked by sliding infantry. W. L. White, '12, broke away from his competitors and bounded over the spruce pile at the bottom of the steep ascent. D. E. Adams, '13, proved to be more skillful with his fingers however, and picked his way to the top of the hill a little faster than Baldwin and White, the race finishing in that order.

COBB MAKES EXCITING FINISH

The cry that A. T. Cobb had been sighted brought the crowds again to the foot of the ski jump, and an ovation was given him as he came speeding over the hill, having raced through the four miles in 23 minutes, 56 seconds; Bache-Wiig, '15, came next; C. E. Shumway, '13, third and "Jack" Bowler, '15, finished fourth, gamely completing a hard race.

This completed the afternoon's regular program of sports, but a treat was offered by the ski men who lengthened their jumps after the run-way had frozen. F. H. Harris, '11, once cleared 57 feet in excellent form and "Dickie" Bowler made 46½ feet.

In the evening came the big social event of the Carnival, the Outing Club dance, and the hall was transformed into a mass of forest greenery. Whole trees, firs, pines and hemlock, stood about the room, while the walls were practically concealed by rough branches. About the walls and floor all the impedimenta of camp life and apparatus of winter sports were displayed. In one corner a small tent was pitched, and the whole room seemed rather a bit of forest than a ball room.

A large white screen framed in fir branches

Watching the Ski-Jumping

aroused the curiosity of the guests until intermission, when an entertaining set of slides illustrating many of the trips and activities of the Club was shown. Some of the slides depicted landscapes on the trails which the Club has followed, views of the White Mountains covered with snow, glimpses of the wild boar and buffalo in Corbin Park, and most amusing of all, snapshots of

"Are You Ready?" "Get Set!" "Go!"

Finish of Snowshoe Obstacle Race

members of the Club in attitudes quaint and curious.

The dance orders contained many characteristic touches in the naming of the dances; the names of some of the dances were "The Hockey Wrinkle," "The Toboggan Slide," and "The White Mountain Bear;" while particularly noticeable among the two-steps were the "Moccasin Hop" and the "Outing Club Trip," while one schottische was called "The Ski Jump." A particularly apropos suggestion was the naming of the dance preceding supper, "The Starvation Roll."

Altogether the dance was considered a great success, and the committee responsible for the arrangements received many congratulations.

On Saturday, the program opened with the ski and snowshoe dashes at the Golf Links. Many amusing spills were taken by the contestants in their anxiety to make speed. An interesting feature was the fact that a Southerner, "Joe" Cheney, hailing from Orlando, Florida, was the successful competitor in the 220 yard ski-dash.

The big card of the whole Carnival, the ski-jumping contest, then took place and from start to finish there was no lack of excitement. Scarcely a second went by without a jumper hurling himself into space off one cr the other of the jumps. The junior jump was won by John Dinsmore. In the novice jump, G. F. Fox, '13, was successful with Bache-Wiig a close second. The senior jump found two old rivals, Cobb and Harris, competing against each other. Cobb had won the college championship twice. This time it was Harris who scored the greatest number of points, his total being 306 to Cobb's 281, but Harris being an alumnus, his score did not count; Cobb therefore won first, with D. T. Rogers, '15, of football fame, only a point behind, with a score of 280 to his credit.

At the conclusion of the afternoon's events, the prizes were courteously presented to the twenty-two winners by Mrs. E. F. Nichols at Dartholme. In the evening, at Webster Hall, came the presentation of the Dramatic Club performance, "The Importance of Being Earnest," which officially brought the Carnival to a close.

So successful was the Carnival, that it has been suggested that Junior Prom be changed to come at this date, and it would seem that this in time may be brought about. The faculty particularly are favorable toward this change, and a week's vacation between the semesters is even promised if this can be done.

Certain it is that if Junior Prom came in the winter, it would not break up the continuity of the college work just at that time when most concentrated thought should be given to preparation for final exams. Furthermore, it would not as now so seriously compete with Commencement festivities.

Coming after the hard grind of Mid-Year's, both the students and the faculty would be only too glad to relax for a few days and all enter actively into the spirit of a Winter Carnival. Permission should not be granted to students to leave town, however, for this would leave the college only half alive and the guests of the college would not see her at her best.

All in all, there seem to be many arguments in favor of the joining of forces by the Outing Club and the Junior Class to work together for this winter event.

In the spring the college is beautiful: so are many other colleges, but in the winter, Dartmouth has a setting which is second to none.

"They're Off"   Start of Ski Cross Country

The present season the Club has enlarged its activities. More men have been off on the trips than ever before, which is a most wholesome sign. The membership has shown a decided increase.

The Carnival, with its winter meet, Outing Club dance and attendant festivities, is planned on a larger scale than before; and right here and now, a hearty welcome is extended to alumni friends and all lovers of winter sports to attend and help make successful the third Winter Carnival to be held during the middle of February.

The big trip of the season, that to the White Mountains, is now an annual affair. It is coming to be the feeling that no man should graduate without taking this trip at least once and oftener if possible.

The trip will probably come the last of February, or the first of March. Part of the time will be spent on the lower levels, where the scenery is more varied and the snow conditions better than above the timber line. It is probable, however, that a definite, well organized attempt will be made with creepers and ropes to gain the summit of Mt. Washington. Arrangements are to be made if possible whereby permission may be obtained to use the Stage Office at the top so that a fire may be built and the climbers may have a chance to rest and get warm before the descent is made.

If the snow conditions are good, a party of the ski men will probably make several descents down Mt. Washington on the old carriage road from the Half Way House to the Glen House. This four-mile slide was made last winter on skis in 15 minutes, and offers an attraction which no ski-runner would willingly miss.

On this and similar trips, the men are taught the

courtesy and natural helpfulness of the trail and are impressed by the lesson which nature has to teach them. They are schooled in that optimism of the Out-of-Doors which makes for the happiness of others as well as themselves, and in the thrift and expediency which emergency demands. Their physical activities teach them self-reliance, while giving them joy and health. In

A Mid-Day Meal in the Dead of Winter

this way every characteristic of strong manhood is given a chance to express itself in the zest of healthy competition or the hardships of the trail. There are moral as well as physical advantages and far distant as well as immediate benefits. While building strong physiques for themselves, the cross-country "hikers" are providing for happier possibilities for the generations

to come.   In this, more than in any other way do the
men come really to

> " * * * have the still North in their hearts,
> The hill winds in their breath
> And the granite of New Hampshire
> Made part of them 'till death."

If you enjoy Nature's single beauties as we find them
in the woodland paths, with the mosses and rocks, and
the pine needles and the flowers, if you like to conquer
some high, rugged, storm-gored peak, if you like to
push your canoe through the placid waters of some
mountain lake under glorious sunset skies, or in winter
turn your skis homeward across a vast frozen expanse
of white as the pink glow in the west grows fainter; if
you enjoy these things, my friend, you are in sympathy
with the hopes and ideals of the Outing Club.   If you
love the sports of the open, if you like to radiate that
something which comes only from the superlatively
healthy, if you like to feel a steady flow of strength
through your body, and warm, pulsing, invigorating, red
corpuscles in your blood, adding new vitality to your
being, and if each year you would like to see more and
more people interested in these things, and enjoying
them you will understand the purpose of this book.

FRED H. HARRIS.

Dean's Office,

Dartmouth College, Hanover, N. H.
Charles F. Emerson, Dean

July 12, 1912.

I am convinced that there is a demand for such a club as the Outing Club in Hanover. The place and the times call for something of this nature in the winter to induce the young men to enjoy to the full the scenery of this part of the country. If rightly conducted, outdoor sports would be an advantage to all concerned. The opportunities in this region for skiing, tobogganing, snowshoeing and other winter sports can hardly be surpassed.

Respectfully yours,
　　Charles F. Emerson,
　　　　Dean of Dartmouth College.

HANOVER, N. H., October 1, 1912.

I consider the formation of the Outing Club one of the most important student movements of recent years in Dartmouth College. The idea of bringing together the men who love the hills and the hill sports, of sending them out into this splendid country, of exploring the near-by mountains, of visiting occasionally the White Hills that are hardly out of sight from the college, of making the most of the glorious Hanover winter with its sparkling air and inviting stretches of snow, of bringing our friends together for the wholesome Winter Carnival,—all this appeals to me as a New Hampshire boy and a Dartmouth man. My own membership in the Club has brought me so much pleasure in the long snowshoe tramps, the comradeship with some of the most manly men of the college, and the better knowledge of the home hills, that I am profoundly grateful to the men who conceived the plan of this Club and so successfully put their plan into effect.

Cordially yours,

CHARLES D. ADAMS.

What Winter Sports
have done for me

By a Southern Man, J. Y. Cheney, '13

IT was my first sight of snow! For more than a month I had waited anxiously for the first fall of snow to come, and when one morning I looked out and saw the ground and trees all covered by a thin, white blanket, I knew that the sight for which I had been waiting all my life had come at last.

I was then a freshman and, although I had heard much of the wonders of snow, I had never had an opportunity of seeing any; so this first slight fall, which foretold the coming of a long winter, was indeed memorable for me. But little did I realize then the full importance of the entrance of snow into my life, and indeed, after the last patch of white had melted away the next spring, I still looked upon it as a mere curiosity and knew but little of the joys and pleasures which it held in store for me, and which, had it not been for the Outing Club, I might never have found. To be sure, I went out on snowshoes a few times, but that was all that it amounted to, and I later found that I knew almost nothing about real "Winter Sports."

In the fall of my sophomore year I joined the Outing Club and went on several of the trips, which marked my awakening to the fact that the long New Hampshire winters, instead of being dreary and tiresome, can easily be made enjoyable and fascinating by simply taking advantage of the opportunities which they offer. I went on snowshoes that first year, but I always admired skis (and envied the ski runners), and several times I tried them, but with little success. However, I did not give up, and after having several talks with President Harris I resolved to learn to use them. Accordingly, when the snow came after Christmas the next winter, it found me prepared to take up skiing in earnest. I had had a little practice the year before, but never with a good pair of skis or fastenings, and I found that this was the principal reason why I had had such poor success. With a good outfit I soon discovered that skiing is actually a sport for every one and not for experts

A Halt for Lunch

only. Of course, like all beginners, I had a great many spills and did not have good "form," but it was not very long before I was able to go on the trips and keep up as easily, and often more easily, than I could on snowshoes.

But this article is not to boost the advantages of skis as compared with snowshoes; it is to boost the advantages of either skis or snowshoes as compared with neither. Although I think skis superior to snowshoes, there are a great many who have tried both and still prefer the shoes, so it is simply a matter of preference, as they both serve the same purpose. It makes little difference which is used; the main object is to use one or the other and to get out and enjoy nature. For the beginner, snowshoes are preferable, because they are very easy to manage the first time out, but after they have been tried and the "fever" caught, skis can be substituted. On the other hand, if a man starts out with skis for the first time, without knowing what he is taking up, he will very likely be disappointed and thus abandon the sport and with it one of the greatest opportunities of his life at college. I say one of the greatest opportunities, because in my estimation the winter sports are the greatest opportunity which is open to many of the men, for there is no other time in a man's life when he is so well able to take advantage of such an opportunity as while at college. During the long winter months there is not much else to do for recreation, and the winter sports afford a means of diversion which is helpful both physically and mentally, and at the same time extremely enjoyable. Yet there are a great many men who, either because they do not care for outdoor activities or because they have no initiative to start them, have let this call pass unheeded and have complained of the monotony of the long, cold winter.

It is to give these men a chance to realize their opportunity and to give them a way in which to take advantage of it, that the Outing Club was formed, and this is exactly what it has done for me as well as for many others. The Club has been formed only three years, but its growth and influence have been very great, owing to the fact that it fills a much needed want;

it is hoped that it will not be long before its membership will include nearly the whole student body as well as the faculty, and that, through its power, Dartmouth will become even more than it is now, the "College of Winter Sports."

Beginner's Form

The White Mountains
in Winter

By David E. Adams, '13

THE OUTING CLUB was starting on its annual "peerade." Mountaineering was in the air. The station platform was crowded with knapsacks and snowshoes and men. Anticipation of sport to come, and relief at relaxation from dull care, shone on every face. The long ride to Gorham passed quickly, and it was a jolly crowd that piled into the big sled en route for the Glen House. In ten minutes the keen mountain air had put a razor edge on every appetite, but, alas, that prospective hot supper was doomed to long delay. If the crowd were mildly surprised at the depth of the snow as it appeared along the tracks in Gorham, they were astonished at the drifts they found just outside. From the first the four big horses had their hands—I should say their feet— full in keeping themselves and their load on the beaten track. Their task was made no easier by the fact that the whole crowd, afraid of being dumped, was perched on the tops of the seats. Twice the sled rolled over into the drifts and had to be extricated by the united efforts of all hands. The first time, the lantern was smashed. The next time, the lead-chain broke at the end of the pole and the leaders started back for Gorham, but Jack Dellinger leaped valiantly to the rescue, and swam back with them through the drifts. A pocket flash was the only light on hand for repairing damages and reharnessing, but the job was done at

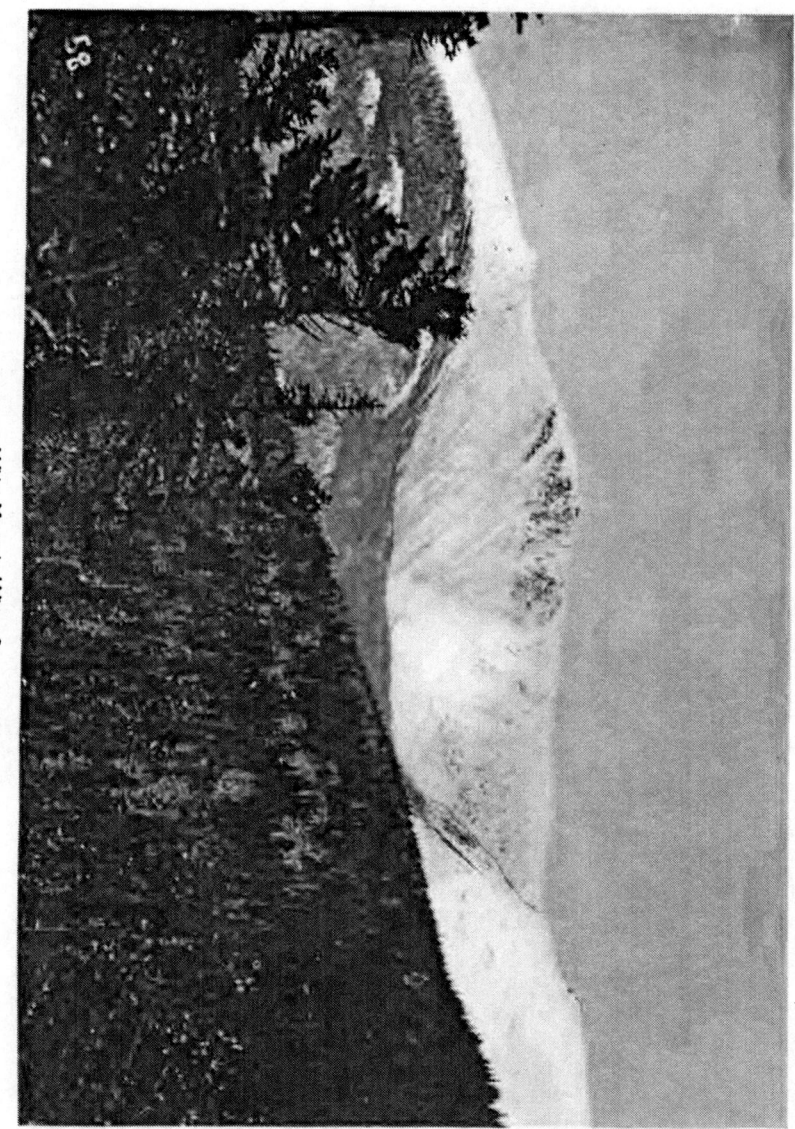

White Mountain Winter Scene

last. After sundry false alarms, the crowd finally pulled into the Glen House about ten o'clock. Supper was most welcome, and even the cool demeanor of the charming waitress failed to daunt the gustatory courage of the jovial "Doc."

The mountains were partly capped next morning, but the sun was bright below and the day boded well for a

The Jovial "Doc"

successful trip into the Great Gulf. The first pull to the Half Way House on the carriage road proved hot work, although the snowshoeing was very good after the first mile. At the Half Way House a split occurred. Four men had determined to attempt the summit of Washington, and after an hour's rest and preparation they roped themselves together, and armed with creepers and picks pushed up the side of the mountain, following the telephone poles. The wind and snow made a dangerous combination to face, and toward the end of the seventh mile, frozen faces warned them to turn back.

Meanwhile the rest of the party had experienced an eventful descent into the Great Gulf. A hard crust made footing impossible, so the only alternative was to sit down and slide. The descent was rapid, to put it mildly, and anyone who had felt chilly from sitting in snow-drifts was soon entirely warm from friction, and lucky if he had any trousers left at all. Below the tree-line the drifts were very soft and deep, and breaking trail proved hard work. The ski men in particular had their difficulties in getting into the gulf. Dinner was served at the Great Gulf Camp, hot tea and ice-water being prominent on the bill of fare. Paper-bag lunches from the Glen House disappeared rapidly. The snow-storm was closing in thick, and the cold was intense, so that the idea of going up the Head Wall was abandoned. The ski men followed the river-bed, with some interesting slides, while the snowshoe contingent took the regular trail down the river. While endeavoring to slide a bank, our doughty chaperon took a header which gave him, for the remainder of the trip, the distinguished appearance of a battle-scarred veteran. Not long after the arrival at the Glen House, Shumway, leader of the summit party, made his rapid descent on skis from the Half Way House by the carriage road. His time was 16 minutes, closely approaching Fred Harris' 14 minute record of the previous year.

Owing to domestic difficulties which caused a shortage of help, our honored president accepted the position

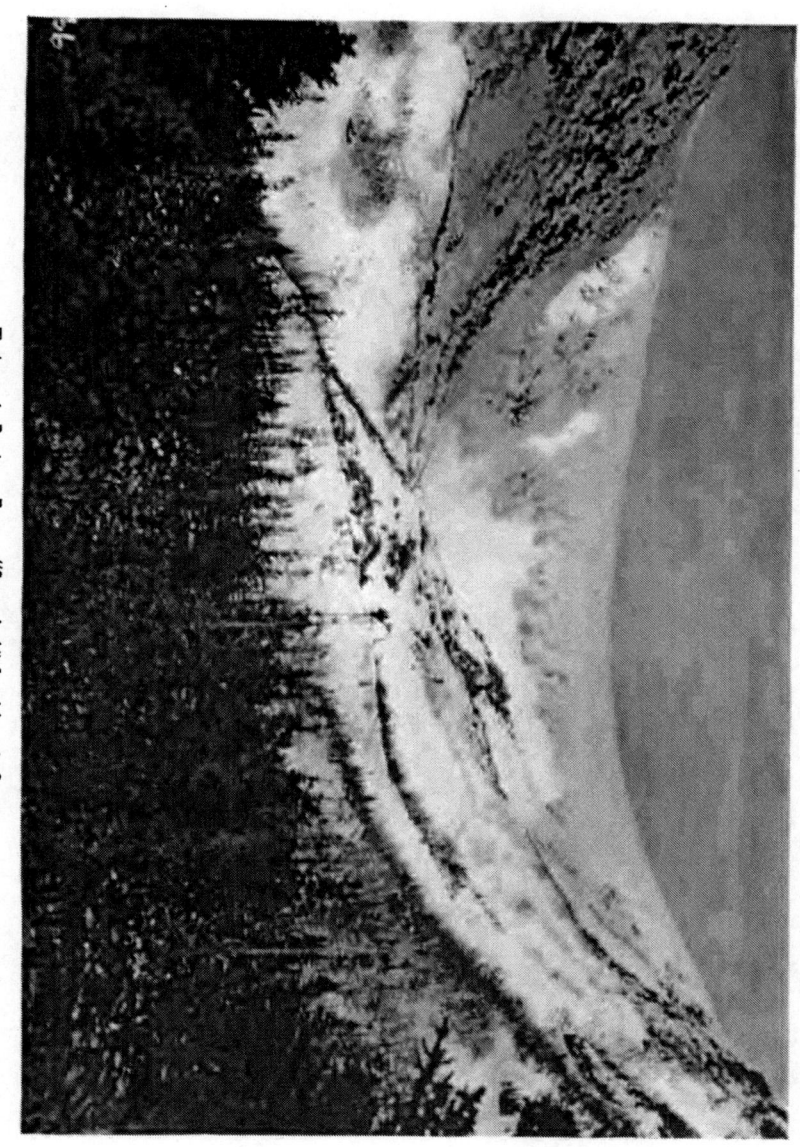

Tuckerman's Ravine. Famous "Snow-Arch" found here in Summer

of assistant hash-slinger, and although not as popular as his fair contemporary, was of material assistance in feeding the hungry horde. A select committee attended to the minor detail of washing dishes.

A most enjoyable evening followed, enlivened by frequent renditions of choice selections from grand opera (a la phonograph). "Nix on the Glowworm, Lena" was the acknowledged success of the evening, and Shumway was so entranced with the selection, that he called up a fair cousin in Gorham, and held the

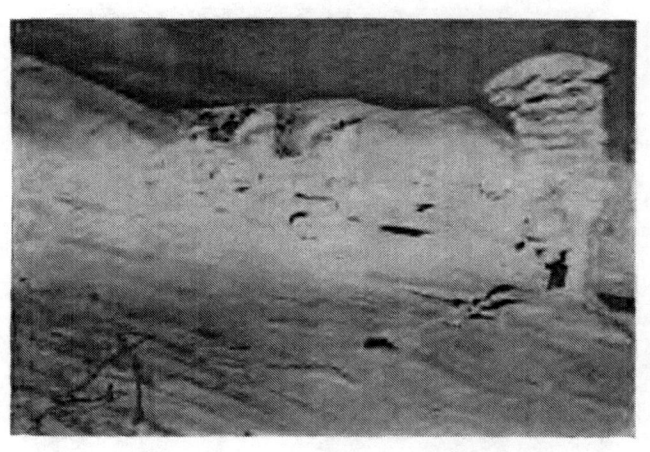

Telephone Poles Near Summit of Mt. Washington

receiver so that she could hear the enchanting strains, greatly augmented by enthusiastic chorus and comment from the entire company.

From the time when, on Monday morning, the first rays of the sun touched the clear profile of the range, the day was absolute perfection. Not a cloud veiled the crystal clearness of the peaks, and not a breath of wind stirred the snow-laden boughs in the valley. The climb to the entrance of the Raymond path was made together. At that point two of the summit party of the previous day with one new recruit pushed on and successfully achieved the goal of their desire. They reported a wonderfully clear view, and almost perfect

An Outlook toward Tuckerman's.

weather conditions, save for some wind, at the top.

The snowshoe contingent entered the Raymond path en route for Tuckerman's. The snowshoeing was ideal, the sun among the spruces gave abundant opportunity for effective use of the camera battery, and altogether the tramp from the carriage road to the Hermit Lake Camp, with occasional glimpses of the Ravine in the distance, was one of the most beautiful in the history of the Club. A very cold wind sucked down through the Ravine, and the noon-day halt at Hermit Lake was necessarily brief. The cold made it impossible to sit still for many minutes, and even in a brief period, "Doc" froze firmly to a frying pan which he had pre-empted as a chair. A "grand right and left" (chiefly for the benefit of the cameras) started circulation again, and the party pushed up the Ravine. Half an hour's hard climbing brought them to the floor, and White and Cheney went several hundred feet up the wall. The great ravine, with its beetling masses of ice and snow, was an awe-inspiring spectacle; and the view of the Carter Range from its floor was magnificent. Return was made by the picturesque trail down the mountain-side via Crystal Cascade, and a tired, happy and hungry crowd met the summit party at the Glen House. Another jolly evening followed, largely occupied by "Lena and Her Concertina."

Monday forenoon saw the whole crowd tramping across to the Ravine House by the Pinkham Notch road, where one of Mrs. Bridgeman's delectable lunches awaited them. Even Mr. Bridgeman's enticing promise of egg-nog could not silence the call of duty, and the noon train bore the majority of the party back to the tame routine of the college campus.

The trip was thoroughly successful. The expense was scarcely beyond the reach of the most modest purse, and the enjoyment far ahead of any trip of its kind.

Every man received a new appreciation of the winter beauty of the mountains, a stimulating and exhilarating change, and a determination to go again.

THE MOUNTAIN AGAIN

The following letter written shortly after the White Mountain trip, when the writer was full of the spirit of the mountains, shows in an intimate and enthusiastic way the enjoyment to be had from winter outing. It describes the trip from the ski-runner's point of view and gives a vivid account of the successful assault on the summit, a feat which, by no means easy in summer, becomes in winter, hazardous in the extreme. Such a letter can not fail to awake the enthusiasm and optimism of all red-blooded men and women.

CROSBY HALL, HANOVER, N. H.,
March, 1912.

"Yes, I went on the Mt. Washington trip and had one peach of a time. I left here Friday, a day earlier than the rest of the bunch. That night I stayed at my cousin's in Gorham, N. H., and after supper eighteen of us, fellows and girls, went on a sleigh ride eight miles up to the Glen House. It sure was some fun, as we didn't return to Gorham until 3 A.M., stopping at the Glen House for a feed and a hum.

Saturday night I met the bunch of fourteen fellows at the Gorham Station, with two sleighs. Lee and I rode over to the Glen House in the double sleigh with two other men, as we could not all get in the big sleigh. We reached the Glen nearly an hour sooner, tipping over but once.

Saturday morning we started at 8.30. Watts, Foster, Fellows, Cheney and I went on skis. We all went up the wagon road to the Half Way House, the best time being one hour and three quarters by both snowshoe and ski men. Then all, except "Pete" Seidler, "Jack" Dellinger, "Les" Little, and I, followed "Doc" Licklider down into the Great Gulf. We four

Short Halt before branching off on path to Tuckerman's Ravine

roped ourselves together, twenty-five feet apart, strapped on ice creepers, and armed with hatchets, stakes, and a half pick-axe, made an assault on the top. A heavy snow was falling when we left the Half Way House.

En Route

We followed up the wagon road to the telegraph poles, then kept to the poles, reaching the two mile post in one hour and a half. We kept on fifty minutes after that, but as the storm had turned into a blizzard and it had become extremely windy and cold, three of us froze our faces. One of the fellows was practically exhausted, having to rest every few

"We Roped Ourselves Together"

minutes, and another was not far from being tired out. As this looked bad, we turned around and started back. At times it was snowing so hard that I couldn't see

Dellinger less than twenty-five feet behind me. We reached the Half Way House again around 3.45 and then had our lunch, thawing it out on the stove. I left the house on skis at 5 o'clock, but for the first half mile it was bad going, as there was a glare crust in which you wouldn't sink at all. Thus when I would strike the curves and start to turn around them my momentum would slew me right off the road into the trees, unless the curve sloped in, so holding my momentum. This caused me to tumble three or four times before reaching that steep side slide, where you looked off down towards the Glen House. I think that was just a little below where you started from last year, wasn't it? I reached there at 5.02 and from there to the bottom of the road I was just sixteen minutes, or eighteen from the Half Way House to the bottom. I tumbled five times but the snow seemed to be faster than last year as it had thawed partially the day before and then frozen. That night we all sat around, swapping stories, and playing the phonograph.

Next morning (Monday) we woke up to find a perfect day, not a cloud in the sky, and the mercury at about 20 degrees. The temptation was too great for me, so "Jack" Dellinger and I planned to make another try for the Summit, also getting George Watts. The whole party kept together up to the two mile sign, where all, except us three, turned off and went over into Tuckerman's. We were on skis, "Jack" having "Eric" Foster's, who had hurt himself the day before running into a tree. We all reached the Half Way House in an hour and a half, or fifteen minutes better than the best snowshoe time of the previous day. Left there at 12 o'clock and kept right on plugging (on creepers of course) until we reached the Tip Top House at 2.05 P.M. Talk about your views! Words cannot describe the grand view we had in every direction. The Tip Top House was one mass of ice and snow on the outside, and inside it was entirely covered with large frost stalactites. Maybe it wasn't beautiful in there! All I could think of was a large cave I once went through in Colorado, which resembled it greatly. After eating lunch, "Jack" got a fire started in the stove, and we warmed up a little as there was a heavy wind blowing up there on top.

The Summit at Last!

Meanwhile I had been snapping a number of pictures, and I expect to get some good ones, as the light was fine. At 4.05 we left the top, and in just one hour we had reached the Half Way House again. In places it would be so steep going down that we would let one fellow slide to the end of the rope, then the next one and so on, two fellows always having firm footing to hold the shock of the third. It sure was sport. The previous day, however, I nearly gummed the fine workings as Seidler and Little got to slipping together, their momentum being so great as to yank Jack off his feet. I hadn't obtained a good foothold before my rope straightened out and so I came cannonballing down into the bunch of them. By good luck they had time to roll out of the way before I connected with any of them.

After reaching the Half Way House Monday we all came down on skis, Wattsie doing it in something like

Tip Top House

nineteen minutes from the slide. The snow was much faster, and although I fell two or three times more I came down from the House in seventeen minutes, and from the slide in a fraction over fifteen minutes.

Tuesday we left the hotel at 8.45 and did the eight miles across to the Ravine House. In order to show the superiority of skis, I reached there about twenty minutes at least before anybody on snowshoes, and a few minutes behind me were Watts and Cheney respectively both on skis. All three of us had packs and snowshoes on our backs, too. Mr. and Mrs. Bridgeman inquired for you. They gave us a fine dinner, after which all except two or three left on the 1.00 o'clock train, having a wait of three hours at Wells River, and getting back here about 8.00 P.M.

The two week-ends previous to this trip I spent over on Moose Mountain, climbing it on one of the days and obtaining a grand view.

The snow is rapidly leaving us now, as it has been thawing since we got back. I sure hate to see it go. Remember how late we were out last year, April 4th; I doubt if we ever equal it again.

Write soon, and let me know what you are doing with yourself.

Ever   sincerely,

C. E. S.

(The following extract from a letter by Lee White, President of the Club in 1912, gives an interesting account of a little incident in Tuckerman's Ravine.)

We sure did have a wonderful time on the trip.   The Glen House accommodations were more than we expected, (as good as the Ravine House), and Monday was one of the finest days that I've ever been out-of-doors. Tuckerman's Ravine was wonderful.   After getting up to the floor of the Ravine, it was very difficult climbing the remaining quarter mile to the head wall, where, in the late spring and early summer, the noted "Snow-arch" is.   Most of the men gave up trying the open way on the crust and took to the rocks on the side of Washington, where they got into a bad fix. I cut a sharp stake and by use of that got up the worst slopes, and Joe Cheney after me. The two of us got

Rough Work Near Tuckerman's

up to the snow-arch and had a wonderful slide back for a quarter mile, besides getting some good pictures. The rest of the crowd got messed up in the rocks and ice and didn't get all the way up, but they had some fine views from where they were.

As ever,

W. L. W.

Hanover and Outdoor Life

By J. W. Goldthwaite

DARTMOUTH COLLEGE without its picturesque natural environment would be a strange place indeed. Take away from it the background of the New England hills, and leave buildings, books, illustrious alumni, and all the old traditions, and the picture yet lacks its most attractive and characteristic colors. No wonder that the Dartmouth man is a man of vigor and action, who enjoys bodily as well as mental exercise; for he has spent four of the best years of his life in a country where one cannot stay long indoors. Here Nature calls from every direction; and often, it must be admitted, she tempts a fellow away from his studies. "Cutting" classes is naturally the most prevalent sin among undergraduates at Dartmouth; and yet if not indulged in to excess such pursuit of wholesome outdoor recreation is of immeasurable benefit to a man and binds him close to his *Alma Mater*. The clear invigorating air of the frosty fall and the crisp white winter, the ennobling beauty of the hills which varies so completely with the seasons, yet is forever tempting a fellow to climb farther and higher for a more extended view; the New England hill farms with their rocky pastures, their old apple orchards, and snug little farm houses; these and many other elements in the environment of the college contribute to make a man's Saturday afternoon outings and holiday camping trips occasions which he will remember all his life.

The topography of the region around Hanover is

Hanover Winter Scene

peculiarly diversified.   Such a variety of land forms, such a display of hills and valleys of all sizes is seldom found.   On every side of the college, within ten minute's walk of the campus are the "vales,"—small winding valleys of dendritic pattern, which intermittent brooks have carved out from the flat, clay plateau that

Follow the Leader

once stretched far and wide over the valley.   Here on the steep banks of the deeply intrenched Connecticut and its tributaries one finds in winter innumerable precipitous slopes down which to slide on skis or snowshoes, and natural winding gorges through which a toboggan whisks and turns as if on a Coney Island scenic railway. When a January thaw has formed a stiff crust on the snow blanket which covers these miniature valleys, the ascent of a short hillside requires much energy and skill, as the gyrations of any novice on snowshoes or skis will testify. Ski jumping here seems the most natural and easy sport imaginable, until a trial of it shows the beginner that proficiency comes only when he has ceased to count spills and bruises. When at the close of the long winter the ravines seem to become suddenly transformed from great icy canyons into little flower-strewn hollows, they cease to call forth the best efforts from an able bodied man. He turns now for exercise to the hills that overlook the valley. But he will not altogether forget the vales, for in them he has discovered a score of different forty-five minute walks for days when time is not available for longer outings.

Equally close to the threshold of the college is "the" river. Here between the pine-covered ridge and the Norwich border farms it flows southward towards the sea, beckoning to restless spirits today as it beckoned to the adventurous John Ledyard in Revolutionary days, when he chopped out his great wooden canoe from the pine tree on the river bank and drifted down to Hartford. Unlike the classic John, however, the modern Tom, Dick or Harry leaves his Ovid and his Greek testament (if he has one) in Fayerweather Hall and satisfies himself merely with food and blanket and the other unintellectual necessities of a week-end camping trip. Paddling up-river to camp out over night is a form of "peerade" in which nearly everybody indulges at least once during his four years in Hanover. And the old swimming hole up by Girl Island is a joyous place on many a hot June day.

The hilly upland that overlooks the valley can best be

appreciated when seen through the eyes of a newly registered freshman, who sets out on his first Sunday afternoon to climb the highest hill he can see. Choosing a road that ascends from the plain and disappears among the rocky hills, the freshman proceeds on his first local journey of discovery with an increasing knowledge of his physical limitations in hill climbing and a rapidly increasing sense of the reality of that quality known as perseverance. Arrived at last with great self-satisfaction at the hill top, he finds at the first glance that in every direction save that of the campus there are other hills, many of them higher than the one on which he stands. Here is food for thought. By the time he has fully considered the situation and has turned to go home he will have come to realize that within a five mile radius of the college there are hills enough to occupy his Sunday afternoons and most of his free Saturdays for all of freshman year. Thereupon he will probably resolve that one hill a week will be his record. Of course he fails to fully carry out this resolution, in the distracting weeks of the football season and the chinning season which follow; but he will nevertheless get out on the hills again about as often as the primitive desire to explore and discover seizes hold on him.

Few country districts are as full of roads as that around Hanover. The pastures and woods are tightly ensnared in a network of them. There are good roads and bad roads, dusty roads and rocky roads, roads bordered by prosperous farms and roads that vanished from the map a century ago and have only stone walls and cellar holes to mark their courses. And yet all are alike in two respects: they show a reckless disregard for hills and they lead nowhere in particular. Within five miles of the college there are approximately one hundred and fifty miles of country road. Likewise, within an afternoon's walking distance are the wayside villages of Pompanoosuc, Hanover Center, Etna ("Etny" let us spell it), Dothan and Jericho, not to mention the more pretentious centers of industry like Wilder, Lebanon and "the Junc." Although these roads, for the most part, are lonely country cross roads, they are pretty well punctuated with those signs of New England thrift

Oh! Who Will Walk a Mile With Me Along Life's Merry Way?
—Henry Van Dyke

and Yankee industry, the "general store," the blacksmith shop, the cider mill, the old town hall, the white church, and the district school. Among these roads is one of peculiar historic interest,—the old Wolfeboro road or College road, which was laid out in 1761 by King George's governor, John Wentworth, to serve as a connection between Hanover and the outside world,— not the world of nature, mind you, but the world of culture and of human affairs. In the dark years of revolution which followed its construction, when the provincial governor was driven away from the land which he had begun so ambitiously to develop, the college road was neglected. The forest was allowed to creep across it and conceal its unused stretches; and the plough soon erased other pieces of it, where newer roads, more obedient to the dictates of topography, afforded easier paths for the farm wagon if not for the horseback rider. Today, instead of serving as a highway from the college out to the civilized world, the old Wolfeboro road serves as the most direct path to the back woods,—the trail over to the Outing Club cabin at Moose Mountain.

And still, this rich supply of hills and country roads for short local trips afield is not all that one finds at Hanover. We must not forget the beautiful little lakes, only 20 miles away, Lake Fairlee and Morey Lake, so suitable for a trip over Sunday. The crowning feature of the region is the nearness of the higher mountains. It is only an eight mile tramp over the Wolfeboro road to the old triangulation station on Moose Mountain, some 2,500 feet above sea-level. By snatching an early breakfast of oatmeal and coffee and getting the 6.28 train south, one may comfortably reach the top of Mt. Cardigan, eighteen miles away, in Canaan, or the somewhat higher apex of the cone of Mt. Ascutney, in Windsor, down the valley, where the barometer reads 3,500 feet above the sea. A blanket and a well filled knapsack provide all that is necessary for sleeping out over night, if a fellow enjoys roughing it. Cube Mountain in Orford, eighteen miles up the valley and hardly eight miles from Fairlee station, offers a good, all day tramp, a

climb of some 2,500 feet, and a splendid view of the
higher mountains.   The sight of these mountains calls
to mind those words of Hovey:

"Praise be to you, O hills, that you can breathe
Into our souls the secret of your power."

Smart's, in Dorchester, is more of a climb, and
little   known   except   to   hunters   and   fishermen;
consequently, it appeals particularly to seasoned and
experienced trampers.   Moosilauke, with its 4,800 feet
of altitude, by far the highest peak visible from the college tower, can be reached by taking an afternoon train
north and returning late the next evening.   From its
summit one gets a very extended view of the central and
southern portions of the White Mountains.   Even the
Franconia Mountains and the Presidential Range are
within reach of Hanover in a few hours' travel by rail;
and the week-end mid-winter trip of the Outing Club
to Mt. Washington offers sport and adventure to ski
runner and snowshoer that would be hard to match at
any other Eastern college.*

So it is no wonder that a strong Outing Club has
grown up at Hanover.   It was inevitable.   Although
as an organization it needed the active efforts of a few
enthusiastic undergraduates to get it fairly started, its
continued growth is assured.   Hanover is just the right
place for such a Club.   And the alumni, remembering
their four years in the New Hampshire hills, will rejoice
that the outdoor spirit has taken visible form.

*For more detailed information concerning the trips here mentioned see
Part III, "Trails from the Campus."

Cross Country on Skis
to Mt. Moosilauke

By Carl E. Shumway, '13.

AFTER I had long wished for an opportunity to climb Mt. Moosilauke on skis, the chance came when G. S. ("Eric") Foster, '13, and I found that we were to have nearly a week off after finishing our mid-year examinations. As the time drew near, we worked out the route which we expected to take, carefully examined our skis for any defects in straps or wood, and then loaded up a pack bag with all the necessaries.

Mt. Moosilauke lies between thirty and thirty-five miles in a straight line northeast of Hanover. It is one of the largest mountains outside of the group lying close to Mt. Washington, and attains a height of 4,811 feet. The tree line is reached when about one mile from the top.

At last our exams. were over, and on the last day of January, 1912, we strapped on our skis for the start. Our course led us up the river road on the New Hampshire side of the Connecticut, past the barrel stave mill opposite Pompanoosuc, and by lunch time we were a couple of miles from Lyme. After a short rest for luncheon we kept on through Lyme, alternating every half hour in carrying the pack bag, and breaking the trail. In places we found the road practically obscured by the drifted snow; however we were able to average nearly four miles an hour. Late in the afternoon we reached the lower part of the village of Orford and saw on the right the enormous stock barns, where a few decades ago many blue ribbon horses and steers were raised by a wealthy Boston man. From there on it was fine skiing, and we reached Fairlee, Vt., about five o'clock, after having crossed over the old wooden bridge which connects it with Orford. We found accommodations at the Fairlee Inn and retired early, as the twenty miles jaunt had made us somewhat tired.

The next day was perfect: clear and cold. After a hearty breakfast, we wrapped our toes with surgeon's plaster, for we had been troubled a little the previous day by our boots chafing our feet. Then we retraced about a mile of our route down the river, and turned off to the left on the road to Orfordville, having a stretch of long uphill work. Passing through this village, we took the road leading to Wentworth, which carried us up between Sunday and Cube Mountains, the latter rising to a height of more than 3,000 feet. As we began to climb up the road leading over the north end of Cube, we obtained our first view of Moosilauke, a dozen miles away. Soon after this we left the road and went across country, following old lumber trails, until we came to a little place consisting of two houses. From there to Warren we followed the ruts of a sleigh which had gone into town the day previous, and obtained about one and one-half miles of swift coasting. We had our supper at Warren, where everyone took a great interest in our skis, also telling us that it would be impossible to climb the mountain on them, since it had never been done before. After supper we covered the five miles on skis to Mr. Eastman's at the foot of Mt. Moosilauke, under a fine, full moon.

The next morning we got away at quarter past nine,

and after covering about a mile, we came to the road which led to the top. As nobody had climbed the mountain before us during the winter, the snow was unbroken, lying deep and loose. Soon the climbing became so steep that we had to wind straps around our skis to keep from slipping backwards. Although this made it slower going, we had no trouble in walking straight up the road.

All on a Frosty Morning

In about three and a half hours, we reached the tree line where the road strikes the ridge leading to the highest peak about a mile away. A heavy gale was blowing, which caused our windward sides to become incased with ice, as our clothes were soaked with perspiration. As we climbed higher, we got into the clouds, which consisted of snow, the blizzard making it impossible to see more than thirty yards. Finally at quarter after one we reached the Tip Top House, and rested in the lee of it while we ate some of our lunch.

We soon commenced to stiffen up on account of the

intense cold, and accordingly decided to start back. At times, one of us would start sliding down the mountain side through the inability of our skis to cling to the icy crust. When we reached the tree line it became fine going, and in numerous places where there would be long steep straightaway, or gradual curves, we would attain terrific speed only to be thrown at some sharp curve or oxbow. To watch each other come tearing down was certainly a sight, for when we tumbled, the snow, being very light, would spurt high into the air. Now and then one of us would take a "header" and practically his whole body would disappear from sight, merely the ends of his legs and skis showing. So we continued down to Eastman's, where we stopped to warm up, then hastening down to Warren, we covered the five miles in an hour. Here we stopped over night at the Riverside House.

The next day it was not until after eleven o'clock that we finally left the village and made the four miles to Wentworth, where we ate our lunch. From there we continued on nearly to West Rumney before taking a branch road, which kept going up, up, up, until it seemed as if it would never come to an end. We reached the height of the ridge just at sunset, and then coasted down into North Dorchester. After a few inquiries, we found we could put up at the Post Office, a couple of miles further on, but were unable to reach it before dark. A good, old-fashioned "boiled dinner" greeted our eyes when we stepped into the house, and in a few minutes we were busy devouring it.

The following day being Sunday, no one arose early, and it was nearly noon before we once more had the skis on our feet. Our trail lay unbroken through the

Group of Enthusiasts

woods for some miles, and at times we would strike across some pond in order to shorten the distance. Thus we slid along past Trout and Cummings ponds, and close under Smart's Mountain, now and then frightening partridges out from under the snow. In one place we were badly mixed up, as three unbroken roads came together at one point; but we kept circling around until we found the one which led in the right direction, towards Reservoir Pond, near which we ate our cold luncheon in a little hut.

Once again the road began to climb until it reached the watershed of the Connecticut. From the top we had a magnificent view to the westward into Vermont and down the river. A heavy, cold wind now blew in our faces, so we donned all the extra clothing we had in the pack-bag, and then had a series of long coasts, which brought us into Lyme Center about five o'clock. As this village is only ten or twelve miles above Hanover, we decided to continue the journey, and do the trip in five days.

We had hardly got outside of the little town before it became dark. Luckily there was little danger of getting off the right road, and so we continued on gliding through the darkness, every few minutes dropping down some small hill. The sky became overcast, making the night extremely dark, in fact, so much so that we were able to tell when we came to a decline only by feeling our skis start sliding away underneath us. In a few places where the roads would turn, we would go shooting across, only to bring up head first in some snow drift. After striking the river road we found easy going and were able to reach Hanover soon after eight o'clock, having covered the thirty miles in less than eight hours of actual travel.

Ascent to Madison Hut by a Member of the Faculty and his Wife

By Nathaniel L. Goodrich.

LEAVING Hanover at noon, March 2nd, we spent the night at the Ravine House, Randolph. Next morning we started up the Valley Way, intending to make the Madison Hut if possible. The snow was in fine condition on the lower slopes, but as we neared the short trees the coating over an old crust grew thin and progress became difficult. The trail runs along the side of the ravine of Snyder Brook, and we constantly slipped sideways. At last we gave it up and dropped to the bottom of the ravine. Here the snow that was missing above had been piled up in drifts of amazing depth, and formed a splendid open pathway. We reached the Hut easily, but found that to go higher required crampons. At the Parapet there was a superb view of Washington and the Great Gulf, but a bitter wind drove us back to the Hut, where we found a sheltered spot in the sun and had lunch. The scrub fir about the Hut, head high in the summer, was drifted in so deep that we did not until afterwards realize that we must have walked over it unseeing.

Returning, we followed the brook bed nearly to the bottom of the mountain; so deep was the snow that we slid over every one of the many falls and water-slides without a glimpse of water or ice. The trip took only eight hours, and was never hurried. To attempt to describe the beauty of the snow-laden trees and the icy slopes is useless and needless.

Weather and snow conditions were ideal and the climb was no more tiring than in summer.   However,

Madison Huts

the fact that two men who made the ascent that afternoon and spent the night in the Hut reported a temperature of 52 degrees below zero at seven P. M., gives a hint of the lurking risks of winter climbs.

Corbin Park in Winter

By Ray W. Tobey, '12.

THOSE of us who strongly feel the call of the hills had often turned longing eyes to the southward, to the region that, so far as the activities of the Club were concerned, had remained unexplored. A score of times the suggestion of a trip to Corbin Park had been made, but without result. Then the interval between examinations and the beginning of the second semester offered the desired opportunity.

The trip through Corbin Park was made on February 3, by nineteen members of the Club. All assembled at Norwich and Hanover station in time for the 6.13 train. At Lebanon we were met by sleighs which conveyed the party to Meriden, from which place a brisk walk of half an hour brought us to the house of the well-known naturalist, Ernest Harold Baynes.

We gathered at the corner of the piazza while Mr. Baynes pointed out the way to the summit of Croyden Mountain, and gave directions for going down the other side to Central Station. Then, while we were putting on our snowshoes, he unlocked the gate to the park, and with a cheer for Mr. Baynes, we were off.

Most of the way we went in single file. The snow was soft and the walking was not always easy, so we took turns breaking trail. Before we had been five minutes on our way, we caught sight of several deer, and several times we halted to watch others that crossed our pathway. Once we were fortunate enough to see a number of wild boar in the valley below.

In spite of Mr. Baynes' explicit directions, differences of opinion began to arise as to the best way to climb the mountain. Before we reached the summit all had agreed that some other route would have been better, or at least that it could have been no worse. This discovery had first been made by the two men on skis as we laboriously wound our way through a thick growth of young bushes. The rest of us realized it too when we began losing ourselves in snow so soft that it would not bear our weight. The mountain top was a welcome sight,

"Just Below the Summit Lay a Little Cabin"

for it meant that we were through climbing. We perched ourselves on the triangulation station and looked upon a panorama of hills and valleys that amply repaid us for all our labor.

In the shelter of the ledge just below the summit lay a little cabin. There packs were opened, lunches were eaten, and repairs were made on broken snowshoes. Then we put on our implements of travel again and commenced the descent. We had felt sorry for the ski men on the way up; now we envied them as they glided past us down the glistening slopes.

For the second time that day we learned how very easy it is to go the wrong way, especially when no one in the party has been there before. At the foot of the mountain we found a gate and learned from the keeper that we had come down the wrong side of the mountain, that we were still six miles from Central Station. The party here divided. Some must return to Hanover early, so they walked to Windsor and took the train from there. The rest went through the "Notch" and reached Central Station shortly after sunset. There we spent a half hour looking at the deer and buffalo in winter quarters, then we went on our way again.

When leaving the park we passed a load of logs. "Where can we get something to eat?" asked one of the fellows.

"Newport," answered the driver.

"How far?"

"Six miles."

There is little more to say about the walk to Newport. We did little talking on the way. There was no need to talk, for there were eleven minds with but a single thought; we knew that Newport contained a restaurant; the sooner we reached it the better.

The restaurant keeper looked surprised as eleven men filed in and deposited snowshoes, skis, and packs along the wall. A few late eaters looked up from their plates and smiled.

The rest is soon told. When we had eaten oysters and beans to our complete satisfaction, and when our president had persuaded the restaurant keeper that his bill should be forty-five cents not thirty-five, we made our way to the railroad station and the Boston & Maine did the rest.

An Outing Trip of Earlier Days

That the activities of the present Dartmouth Outing Club are in the natural order of the College traditions is suggested by Mr. N. L. Goodrich, the librarian of the College, who has unearthed the following interesting account of an undergraduate expedition led more than *a century ago* by Dartmouth's indefatigable adventurer, John Ledyard:—

" * * * * * In midwinter, when the ground was covered with deep snow, Ledyard collected a party whom he persuaded to accompany him to the summit of a neighboring mountain, and there pass the night. Dr. Wheelock consented to the project, as his heart was bent on training up the young men to be missionaries among the Indians, and he was willing they should become inured to hardships, to which a life among savages would frequently expose them. The projector of the expedition took the lead of his volunteers, and conducted them by a pathless route through the thickets of a swamp and forests, till they reached the top of the mountain, just in time to kindle a fire, and arrange their encampment on the snow, before it was dark. The night, as may be supposed, was dreary and sleepless to most of the party, and few were they who did not greet the dawn with gladness. Their leader was alert, prompt at his duty, and pleased with his success. The next day they returned home, all perfectly satisfied, except perhaps Ledyard, with this single experiment of their hardihood, without being disposed to make another similar trial. He had a propensity for climbing mountains, as will be seen hereafter, when we meet him at the Sandwich Islands."—From "Life of John Ledyard"

By SPARKS, 1829.

"Above the Clouds" or a Summer on the top of Mt. Washington

By Carl E. Shumway, '13

This story and the one following it descriptive of summer life (although even then with a touch of winter in it) in the same field in which we have followed the Club's activities in winter, may not seem out of place at this point.—*Ed.*

ON the 27th day of June, 1912, the stage driver and I drove to the top of Mt. Washington, reaching there soon after sunset. Thus commenced my stay of nearly eleven weeks on the summit of the second highest mountain east of the Rockies.

Many of the days we were shut off from the world below by the clouds, which would oftentimes form around the cone of Mt. Washington, when there was not the least vestige of a cloud in any other part of the sky. However, the clear days well repaid us, and on such days, tourists came flocking to the summit by the cog railroad, in carriages and automobiles on the famous wagon road, or on foot by the numerous mountain paths. It was just such a day that June 30th turned out to be, clear and cold. There appeared to be no limit to one's vision, except where earth and sky seemed clearly to meet. Portland Harbor, the smoke of Bangor, and the far-off Adirondacks could be plainly seen. Such a day is very rare in the summer, but in the winter they are of frequent occurrence, as the air is so dry and cold. The members of the Outing Club were favored by a similar day last winter, when three of its members were able to reach the top on ice creepers.

Oftentimes even during the three summer months the

mercury dropped away down below freezing, while heavy frosts and snow-storms were far from rare. It was in such weather that a number of Hanover friends got caught, Professor Lingley and his wife, Superintendent and Mrs. Hunter, and Mr. Skinner, finding a heavy snow-storm raging when they arose the morning of August third. The storm continued all the morning, some four inches of snow falling. About three weeks

Spalding Lake. White Mountains

later, Registrar Tibbetts with Mrs. Tibbetts and Mr. and Miss Storrs reached the top just before a cloudburst, after which they were fortunate enough to witness one of the most remarkable cloud effects of the summer. During the night the mercury dropped and with it came a storm which drove many trampers from the exposed camps to the top of the mountain. All day long they kept crowding into the Stage Office and the

Tip Top House, until the former had fifty-four persons to accommodate.   By morning the top of the mountain was a mass of ice and frost, the windows thickly frosted, and the water barrel frozen so tight that I had to use an axe to cut it open.   Everyone, however, decided to "take a chance," about forty of the trampers going down the exposed Crawford Trail, on which four persons have lost their lives.

Oftentimes after such a storm the view from the top was most fascinating, only the upper part of the cone protruding from the clouds, and possibly the highest peaks of the Franconia Range and Mt. Moosilauke. As one watched the clouds all he could imagine was a storm at sea, the vast spumy clouds breaking on the storm-gored ridges and rolling up over the rocks like waves.   At times a spiral of cloud would shoot up into the air to a height of thousands of feet, caused by its passing over some very warm spot of the earth, such as a forest fire.   A top of a mountain would appear for an instant through the clouds, and then, like a ship sinking in the hollow between the waves, disappear, only to be apparently thrown to the top of another wave.   But prettiest of all was the sunset, tinging the clouds to pink, and setting off the clear blue sky.   It brought to mind the lines of Robert Service in "The Land God Forgot,"—

> "The lonely sunsets flare forlorn
>   Down valleys dreadly desolate;
> The lordly mountains soar in scorn
>   As still as death, as stern as fate.
>
> The lonely sunsets flame and die;
>   The giant valleys gulp the night;
> The monster mountains scrape the sky,
>   Where eager stars are diamond-bright."

Many afternoons I spent in roaming around the mountains by the numerous trails. One of the prettiest of our trips was down the Six Husbands' Trail Extension, which starts above the tree line, and then drops down through the short, stunted growth by steep pitches, tunneling under an enormous rock. Then it winds across the floor of the Great Gulf, which a party of D. O. C. men explored last winter on skis and snowshoes. Crossing the west branch of the Peabody River the trail climbs up over the knee of Mt. Jefferson, ascending so steeply that we had to cling on with our hands, in two places ladders being used to climb up out of tunnels.

Another day we went down Tuckerman's' Ravine, which together with Raymond path, constitute the two hardest and most dangerous trails in the mountains. The former arises almost perpendicularly, after leaving a rock slide and smooth sloping rock shelf at the bottom. The footing is very treacherous and a misstep would mean that your friends would be sending flowers in a few days. This is probably the best way to ascend if one wishes to get an idea of the great height of the walls and the force that must have been exerted by the glacier in scooping out the ravine.

Later on I climbed up the Raymond cataract, a series of innumerable falls from its source about one-half a mile from the top. There is no trail, and one has to jump from rock to rock, walk under water falls, and climb up the face of the stream until it disappears underground for about a quarter of a mile. Then one is left in a stunted growth which is so thick that a person can walk along the tops of the trees.

It happened that the Dartmouth Geology Party was

up in the White Mountains for six weeks this summer under the charge of Professor Goldthwaite, so we could see each other at times.   The cook at the camp, Lee White, last year's President of the Outing Club, could have been described as,—

"He's gaunt as any Indian, and pretty nigh as brown;
* *
He sports a crop of whiskers that would shame a
healthy hog."

The first day I saw him this summer he appeared like a "knight of the road," as he had just completed blazing a new way from Hermit Lake to the top.   It chanced that the day after Fred Harris won the tennis championship of New Hampshire he came up eight and a half miles over the Crawford Trail to the Stage Office.   It seemed like a reunion when Lee and Professor Goldthwaite climbed up the next noon.

Although the White Mountains are famous as a summer resort, yet there are many spots in them that trampers have seldom been through on account of their inaccessibility.   Each year people attempt climbing to the top in stormy weather, thinking that a storm in the mountains is not different from one below.   This has caused the deaths of eight persons since 1850, who between the months of June and October essayed to climb Mt. Washington.   Even during this summer a number of people were lost, but fortunately other parties found them.   It was a common sight to see persons come staggering into the office and drop the moment they saw they were safe.   One night a party of ten intended to climb the mountain by moonlight, but when they reached the bottom it had commenced raining.   Nothing daunted, they pushed on up the eight miles of wagon road, but reached the top so exhausted that they did not dare to return through the cold driving rain for three of their party who had given out. Luckily there was another tramper at my place, so I routed him out and we followed down the road until we found the group huddled under the rocks.

Unfortunately the weather on the summit during this summer was the worst it has been for years, day after day being clouded in. Many times at night the clouds would settle, or dispel, giving a beautiful view of the surrounding rugged peaks. The large summer hotels and towns seemed like blotches of fire scattered over the country, while trains resembled streams of burning oil. It was while standing on some jutting boulder on a clear night like this that the mystery and weirdness of the lone mountain top would impress its grandeur on me. Only our Alaskan poet, Robert Service, seems to be able to draw vivid descriptions of these wild desolate places, so I fall back on him again through lack of words:

"The land was still and strange and chill, and cavernous and vast;
And sad and dead, and dull as lead, the valleys sought the snows;
And far and wide on every side the ashen peaks arose.

The moon was like a silent spike that pierced the sky right
    through;
The small stars popped and winked and hopped in vastitudes
    of blue;"

Thus the summer passed all too quickly. Although it may be the reader's impression that it must have been lonely there, yet this was not the case. It was only with a feeling of sadness and regret that I drove down off the mountain that September afternoon, not to return again until the next winter.

Reminiscences of a Geological Camp

By the Cook

NOT to detract overmuch from the wonders of our winter sport by too long a summer tramp, I shall venture to allude to a few incidents of a trip into the northern peaks of the Presidential Range of the White Mountains, which may not prove wholly uninteresting to those others, who, like ourselves, can camp in the rain for six weeks and yet find a certain joyous delight in bearding nature at its worst. We started with about two hundred pounds of duffel, one hundred and sixty of which we moved at a trip; the remaining forty generally being the victim of a return journey for one of us. For shelter we had two light balloon silk tents, weighing less than six pounds apiece; the rest of the two hundred comprised our blankets, pouches, axes, clothes, food, scientific instruments and cameras.

We pitched our tents up among the briars and boulders of King's Ravine, not far from the delightful mossy falls. Our purpose was the careful study of traces of local glaciation. Here in King's we were duly discovered by the press agents of the black fly colony and advertised by them as guaranteed under the Pure Food and Drugs Act. We got out an injunction against the tribe in the form of various lotions and salves, resulting as usual in the ruination of everything we came in contact with, excepting the flies. We remained here but four days and I have suspected that our friends with the big sting had quite as much to do with our unceremonious departure as did the lack of scientific phenomena.

Leaving behind us the precipitous headwall of King's, we retreated down valley by the Randolph Path to Snyder Brook, whence we ascended the Mt. Madison trail to Bruin Rock. At this spot we discovered to our sorrow that both banks of the brook presented a thirty degree slope well covered with boulders and caverns.

The Cook

Nothing daunted by this irregular aspect of our intended camp site, our ambitious leader suggested that we call up our steam shovel and derrick and proceed to remove a sufficient mass of the hillside to afford a suitable level spot. In the course of time, by much wielding and dulling of both axes and finger nails, we brought this to pass. Until we were thus rudely forced to slice off several cubic yards of this hillside I had regarded the geological hammer as a useless and bulky encumbrance; a few days later on the top of Madison I found it to be an ideal tool for constructing an approved fire place.

On the summit of Madison we were a mile high and in the immediate proximity of the Madison Spring Huts and their hospitable keepers. Up here we became intimately acquainted with the vicissitudes of the weather man. The first morning we arose to find a mass of icy fog and the temperature at thirty-four. Shortly after breakfast I descended to the Ravine House and found a scorching sun and eighty-five degrees. I reached the top again in a pouring rain, which was reinforced before night by a hurricane of wind that roared across the peaks with a boisterous and vicious frenzy, tearing savagely at our tent ropes. Had it not been for the protection of the neck-high scrub, we should all have parachuted into Berlin, a mile below, on the wings of that rollicking gale.

On such intimate terms with "The Hut," we enjoyed an opportunity to inspect at close range the many people who venture to explore the mountain trails. It is quite amusing to watch some of these at their work— work which should be play. One wonders how any human can bring to the top of Madison the attitude of a furnished flat without smashing it beyond recognition on the rocks below. The eight solid walls of these huts sometimes shelter as diverse accoutrements as moccasins and French heels; silks (quite generally torn) and rough homespun. But it is most often the trampers who have been fairly well and sensibly outfitted by friends, but who are as yet green to the trail, that furnish the greatest source of amusement. Such a party it was who, arriving in a heavy rain, put their soaking woolen clothes into the oven to dry. While this operation was in progress, they robed themselves in army blankets and gossiped with the keepers in the other hut. With sorrow I relate the tragedy. A smell brought them hurriedly back and the opened oven surrendered two half baked buttons, and more smell!

While still on the top of Madison, where, I admit, the sun never had a chance, I fain would inject a word of caution to would-be sunrise friends. I have never, from the summits of some of the highest peaks in Vermont, New Hampshire, and Maine, seen a sunrise or sunset that was comparable to many I have enjoyed from the meanest hillock about home. You are invariably too high up to get the lights and shadows that cause such wonderful effects from lesser heights. And as for the view at sunrise, why, it's infinitely better later in the day.

After more than a week of erratic weather here, we descended to The Ravine House. The others having a considerable start of me that morning, I essayed to run the greater part of the way wherever the trail would permit. Bumping along with my pack-load swinging high over my head, I burst suddenly upon a party of four going up. The first three of the company saw me in time to give room, but the last, a pre-occupied lady, had no idea that a stranger on four legs or two was within a mile of her until I violently brushed her aside in my mad career. Thereupon she broke into frightful shrieks of "Bears! bears!" and sunk upon the trail in noisy hysterics; at which juncture I turned the next corner. I am minded to observe that a wise woman keeps her eyes "peeled" in the woods. *It might have been* a bear.

From the Ravine House our outfit was taken to the Glen House via the Pinkham Notch road by wagon, and here we secured our mail and provisions for the latter half of our trip. It was also here that the curiosity of a Boston gentleman was excited by my hob nails. He thought them a splendid invention for climbing and marveled that he had not been told of them. I secured his blessing by giving him a handful. Our objective point was now Tuckerman's Ravine, which we ascended by the usual route of the Raymond Path via the Mt. Washington carriage road to the two mile post. We happened on a most delightful spot within a cricket chirp of Hermit Lake and on the very bank of an icy mountain torrent. Our eighteen days here were, I think, the most pleasurable part of our trip, in spite of incessant rain and bothersome red squirrels.

The first morning, having coaxed the bold little "reds" up on our breakfast table and almost into the sugar can, we were proud of ourselves as blossoming Hagenbecks, but that noon I was made to eat humble pie. Returning from "The Glen" with a pack of provisions, I discovered much villiany. Unable to penetrate my precautions in other ways, they had eaten through the oiled silk fabric of the "feed tent" and sampled each and every food bag. The supplies I regretted but little, as more were to be had for the hauling, but flour and corn meal bags full of squirrel holes are useful only as sieves. I sought revenge the next day by throwing nine of the robbers into a stew whereat there was much rejoicing in camp until the next morning, when I awoke to find "number ten" peeking at me from over the rim of the oatmeal pot which the night before had held our half-cooked morning's porridge.

The end of our first week in Tuckerman's was enlivened by a visit from Mr. Emerton of the Appalachian Mountain Club, who is commonly known as "Spider," because of his scientific interest in the weavers of webs. His arrival was the signal for the clouds to drop to lower levels, and for two days it poured water, the salvation of the camp being accomplished only by an elaborate system of water works such as would dignify almost any community. The weather being such, Mr. Emerton was pressed to abide with us overnight and did so. I recall that he rested warmly in the folds of a featherlined sleeping bag and that his appearance when he crawled out of it at four-thirty the next morning betokened relationship with other well-known early risers.

When we arrived in Tuckerman's the latter part of July there were still several tons of snow under the shadow of the head wall, but this melted away in the course of our sojourn. In addition to his geographical researches the leader of our party, Professor Goldthwaite, essayed extensive topographical work in this locality, and before we struck camp had added both Huntington and Tuckerman Ravines to Mr. Cutter's invaluable map of the northern peaks.

On Monday, August 5th we were interrupted about supper time by the arrival of two brothers who were stopping at Hermit Lake Camp overnight, and who had come over to discover whether or no we had seen many bear signs thereabouts. They carried ugly looking Colts on their hips and announced that they had served as members of the National Guard. We added to their obvious anxiety by assuring them that bears frequently visited us of a night and were only deterred from invading the tents by the protecting flap of mosquito netting. Thereat we could see they desired to borrow a few yards of netting, but bashfulness overcame them and they left without it.

I had word that on Wednesday, August 7th, our first Outing Club President, Fred Harris, would ascend Washington by the Crawford Path to visit Carl Shumway, President of the Club for 1912-1913, who, as every lady tramper will tell you, was the gracious and obliging host at the Stage House. So, as that day dawned fair, I clothed myself in the cleanest of my woolen shirts and the driest of my boots, with no choice as to trousers, and alone, save for two ham sandwiches and five weeks growth of beard, started for the top. In an hour I was at the Stage House conversing with my one time room-mate Fred, who, after some little talk and much persuasion, was convinced of my true identity, pot-black and all. Imagine if you can my acute dismay when the first train load on the cog railway landed a be-flanneled and be-silked party from the Crawford House, who had come up with their luncheon. With considerable reluctance and with much trepidation I consented to lunch with, but not too near them, and my courage was rewarded later by a very charming young lady, who exclaimed, "Well, anyway, Mr. White, I shall never again be afraid of tramps." Whereat I showed my appreciation by a horrible grin. Prof. Goldthwaite shortly appeared, plane-table in hand, and the four of us had a regular D. O. C. re-union out on the rocks overlookng the Crawford Path and the Lake of the Clouds.

On the twelfth, our scientific work practically completed and the weather continuing bad, we decided to move to the Great Gulf for our last few days. We toted out to the carriage road and sent half of our things down by the stage. Then, with lightened loads, we packed up to the Half Way House and dropped down, via the Mule Trail, to the Appalachian (1910) Camp site, the same route traversed by the Club in March. We pitched our remaining tent in conjunction with the old guide's shack, and found the combination the most satisfactory shelter of our trip.

Mr. John Ritchie, Jr., of the A. M. C., one of the Club's old friends, came up from Boston one day and

"Prof. Goldthwaite Shortly Appeared Plane-table in Hand"

dropped in on us at supper time. I recall that our supper of soup, beans and bacon, potatoes and cocoa, was substantially increased by the contents of our visitor's ruck-sack, which gave up jelly and turkey sandwiches, doughnuts, cheese, boiled eggs, and many other Hub delicacies. I attempted to return the favor the next morning by picking a mess of blueberries and raspberries on the trail out, but Mr. Ritchie had changed his mind and gone on to Washington 'ere I returned.

Bright and early the sixteenth we toted up to the Half Way House, and thence four miles down to "The Glen," where Professor Goldthwaite and Plummer left for Gorham and the train. For myself, I turned back and reclimbed Washington to spend the night with Shumway on top. I found him in a very unsettled state, for forty young ladies of a well-known summer camp had spent the previous night in his 15 x 20 house. It seemed incredible on the face of it, but was satisfactorily attested by the people who run the Tip Top House. By way of getting things in their normal condition, Carl set me to sawing a supply of wood. The next afternoon I went over Clay, Jefferson and Adams via the Gulfside Trail to Madison Hut, where Wallace Pearce, the assistant keeper and I, having prepared supper for two parties of neophytes, played cards well into the night. Sunday, the rain returned with fresh courage and I slipped and slid ungracefully down to the Ravine House, where I arrived soaked to the skin but very happy.

From the vantage ground of October it is a memorable six weeks to look back upon, and the five days that it did not rain loom less large in my recollection than they did. Somehow or other the "long hours of wet" are among the most pleasurable memories, but at the time— well, have you ever cooked for a week in the rain over an open fire?

W. LEE WHITE '12.

The Apparatus of Outing
and how to use it

CONCERNING SKIING

By Fred H. Harris

THERE are many who enjoy the webbed shoe as a means of winter travel, and I readily acknowledge its usefulness. It certainly has its place. It enables you to travel abroad in winter, to penetrate into the forest vastness and brings you in contact with nature's charms at a time of year when otherwise you might be restricted to the beaten and more confined paths of civilization. In this chapter however, I wish to treat of the ski. Whereas the snowshoe simply affords a means of travel and enables one to conquer natural difficulties in winter, the ski not only does this but offers at the same time a wonderfully fascinating sport.

It is sometimes thought that the skis are to be used simply to slide down hill, after which it is necessary to take them off and carry them back up the hill over your shoulder. It is believed by some that whereas the ski is useful in open country, its usefulness ends when it comes to woods or underbrush. This is far from being true. It is possible to strap your skis firmly to your feet and go all the afternoon through thick country and through open, up hill and down, over stone walls and through gullies, and return home without once taking them off, and, what is more, to cover the same distance in shorter time than it would be covered by one who wore snowshoes. There are practically no places where the skis can not be used. You can penetrate the woods with ease and wend your way very rapidly through the trees. There are very few places where the snowshoe is superior to the ski, and the ski is constantly demonstrating its advantage over the snowshoe. No hill is too steep to be climbed on skis

and no descent is too hazardous to be undertaken. There are simple ways of conquering all obstacles which may arise.

True skiing is a sport for men, men who have real red blood in their veins and men who will spend enough time to conquer the difficulties, and who are "willing

When jumping, the watchword is "lean forward"

to take a chance." The reason we have no more ski-runners is that it is so hard to learn the knack of handling the elusive blades at first that many give up in disgust before they have penetrated far enough to discover what wonderful pleasures the sport can offer. Anything worth while comes hard and skiing is no exception. Where one can learn to use snowshoes passably well in a couple of days, it takes at least a year to learn to ski, and there is absolutely no limit to what one can do in the sport. A great deal depends on the way the beginning is made. Suppose we have a crust on the day we commence to learn. Contrary to the general opinion, a crust is the worst possible condition of snow for skiing. Supposing the fastenings are poor and fit badly. Suppose we go at it any old way. Under such circumstances as these I can imagine nothing worse than skiing. But on the other hand, let us suppose the first attempt is made in the company of one who has had experience and that the skis are of the right pattern, the footgear suitable, and a blanket of soft snow covers the ground. Under these circumstances, if one will follow the directions of his instructor and not try to do too much the first day, he is almost sure to become an enthusiastic follower of the sport. There is a right way and a wrong way about everything, and curious to say the things one has a tendency to do in skiing are the very things one should not do. Consequently, if one has no instructor, nor reads any good book on the subject, bad habits are likely to be formed which may prove an effective barrier to the realization of the real beauties of skiing.

One naturally feels that skis can only be used to go in a path approaching more or less a straight line. A friend who was an expert skater once said to me, — "Of course in skating you can make all kinds of curves and fancy figures whereas in skiing you can only go in a straight line," — but you see he had never seen the manoeuvres of an expert on skis. All kinds of curves and swings are possible. By means of a Telemark swing, one can, while going at the rate of forty-five miles an hour, swing with perfect precision at a sharp curve either to the right or left, send up a cloud of snow, and stop

Up Carriage Road on Mount Washington

short within a few yards, facing the hill down which he came. Other useful manoeuvres are the Christiana swing, the kick-turn, stemming, herring-boning, snow-ploughing, and many others. It is indeed a sport which will give pleasure from the very first and yet one which will challenge the best that is within you.

Come with me, if you will, to the ski-jumping tournament, which will offer one of the most spectacular athletic contests you have ever witnessed.

It is in the middle of February and the snow is several

feet deep. The course has been especially prepared and is in fine condition. Many interested spectators throng the ropes on either side, and flags and bunting decorate the scene.

The clerk of the course waves his flag to indicate that everything is clear, the cornetist gives the signal, and number one with the large numeral in black and white pinned to his breast disengages himself from the group at the top of the awful descent, and the start is made. The jumper comes down at an ever-increasing speed. Just before the "take-off" he crouches, and then as the platform is reached, goes through an unrolling process or upward spring known as the "saats," and shoots into the air at a speed of a mile a minute, out, out and then down, down (never up), to land perhaps a hundred feet away on the incline below. If he is fortunate in "standing" he continues forward at high speed to the "outrun," and stops abruptly amidst a whirl of snow in a brilliantly executed Telemark or Christiana swing.

The course is straight away without turn, and to an onlooker watching from near the "take off," the progress of a man from Lilliputian size high in one direction to a rapidly flashing life size figure and on to diminutive proportions far away in the valley below is very interesting and startling.

A ski-jump is usually situated amidst beautiful natural scenery. Surrounded by snow-capped hills against a deep blue sky, the surroundings from the spectator's standpoint can hardly be equalled.

To see a man make this wonderful descent of a thousand or more feet partly on the snow and partly in the air all in a few seconds is a sight never to be forgotten and when the last jumper has made his leap and the tournament is over, the recollection of the spectacle that has taken place before one's eyes is something that will not soon fade from memory.

How to Ski—A Few Suggestions

It is first necessary to secure the right kind of skis; and above all, be sure to have good fastenings. Skiing is too much of an art to be gone at in a haphazard manner, and yet, if a proper outfit is secured and the first trials taken in the right way, it is something that anyone can accomplish. To think that skiing is for a few experts only, is a mistaken idea—it is a sport for everybody.

The proper ski to be used is of the Telemark type, such as the Hagen or Hansen Norwegian skis, or similar American makes, and the proper length is from the ground to the center of the palm when the arm is extended vertically overhead. Some good binding which will permit the foot to move freely up and down, but will allow of no lateral movement at all, is the next thing necessary; the most popular fastenings are of the Huitfeldt or the Hoyer—Ellefsen pattern. Do not be satisfied with a cheap outfit, but get the best to start with. Do not say to yourself: "I will get a cheap pair now, and a better one later, when I have learned how to use them." If you take that attitude, you may never learn. A beginner is handicapped enough without further handicapping himself with an inferior outfit. The best is none too good.

Having secured the proper skis and fastenings, the matter of clothing and shoes is the next thing to consider. Buy a pair of high leather boots a couple of sizes too large so that they may be filled with woolen

EASY THE DESCENT TO AVERNUS.

HEAVN IS NOT REACHED BY A SINGLE BOUND

UNPRINTABLE!!

SNOW-DIVING DOES NOT OFFICIALLY FIGURE AMONG THE EVENTS.

socks. Get a shoe as nearly water-proof as possible; some of the square-toed cheaper variety are better than the high priced fancy articles, and serve very well.

Perhaps the best boot of all is that of the regular Norwegian type such as is sold for about $5.00 by R.& W. Kerr, Ltd., of Montreal, and other firms. In height it comes but a little above the ankle and is light and serviceable. The sole is thick and well-shaped to fit the irons. The back part of the heel is cut in the form of a curve to prevent the back strap from slipping

The Start for the Half Way House

down, which is a great convenience. Sometimes a strap is sewed to the heel to accomplish this same result. If you have neither, a thong attached to the back strap and tied around the ankle will serve very well.

Keep the boots well oiled or viscolized. Do not wear flannel or fuzzy clothes, for, if you do, the snow will stick to them and after a few falls you will resemble an animated snowball. Wear old clothes; a suit of some cloth with a hard finish is best. A sweater is all right if worn underneath, and a blue flannel shirt is a valuable adjunct to your outfit; above all do not put on too many clothes.   Skiing is strenuous enough so that you will be more than warm enough when seemingly lightly clad. Mittens are much warmer and more serviceable than gloves; a heavy woolen pair of the 50 cent "Farmers" variety is one of the most necessary parts of your outfit.

Never undertake to learn how to ski alone if it is possible to go with some one who is more or less an expert in the sport.   You will find that all ski-runners are only too glad to spend time in coaching those who are just beginning.   If you cannot find some friend who is willing to take you out, avail yourself of the advice to be found in some good books and of these the best are "The Ski-Runner," by E. C. Richardson, Secretary of the Ski Club of Great Britain; "How to Ski and How Not To," by Vivian Caulfield, and "Skiing for Beginners and Mountaineers," by Rickmers.

If you undertake to try skiing by yourself, you will in all probability try it under the worst circumstances possible, and gain a very erroneous impression of this great sport.   It is very necessary to get started along the right lines.

Select some day when the thermometer is not higher than 20 degrees Fahrenheit, with soft, fluffy snow on the ground—a hard crust with a fall of several inches on top is the ideal (until the wind comes along and scours the crust bare again) —but this is not often found.

Try going along the level at first, and use a slipping, sliding motion, lunging your weight forward on to the front ski.   It is important to take your weight off the back ski quickly.   This lunge forward ought to make the front ski slide forward a few inches or several feet or even yards, according to the state of the snow or the proficiency of the runner. Just before the forward ski ceases to move, lunge forward quickly with the other ski, and coast, so to speak, on that ski until it nearly comes to rest. You will soon find yourself slipping rapidly over the ground with very little exertion. If the snow be very deep and "slow," you will find that the ski slips forward scarcely at all after you push it forward; but if the snow is "fast" and you do not sink in very deeply, you will sometimes slide long distances with each step. Keep the feet together. A narrow track or "spoor" is an indication of the expert. A wide, wobbly track conclusively indicates a beginner.

A little later try sliding down hill on easy gradients. As on the level, keep the feet together, with one ski slightly ahead of the other. They should make but a single track in the snow. Put the most weight on the ball of the forward foot. Indeed, the phrase "Stand Forward" is the watchword of skiing. You will find that you will scarcely ever fall forward. Nine out of ten times, when you fall, it will be because your feet shoot out from under you and you will fall backwards. You will soon find that it is comparatively easy to maintain your balance, and you can then try some slightly steeper hills.

Do not avoid hill-climbing. Never take off your skis and carry them up hill on your shoulder. Getting up hill requires the most "knack" of all, but after it is once acquired you will cease to worry about hills. Almost anybody can get down hill after a fashion, but it takes an expert to surmount a hill in easy style.

HOW TO JUMP

Do not attempt to jump until you have become more or less proficient in straight running, turning, hill climbing, etc. It is better not to undertake to jump seriously at all the first year.

It is very necessary to find the right kind of a hill before one can think of jumping, and, unfortunately, a really satisfactory hill is something not easily found.

Ready (?) for the Take-Off

The ideal hill consists of a long steep approach which shall give all the speed necessary. The curve from the hill out on to the jump should be a gradual one, and the ground below should fall away sharply at an angle of 30 degrees. The alighting-ground should continue on a steep slope for some distance below the "take-off," gradually growing less steep until it meets the level

"Then follows the hiss of the jumper's body, as it passes through the air"

ground, which should continue for a sufficient distance to provide a suitable "out-run." Remember,—the jump should be built on the steep part of the hill. Never have your "take-off" so near the bottom that the jumper will land on the level or anywhere near it. The jumper needs the alighting place to continue at a steep descent for a long enough distance so that he will have plenty of time to regain his balance before he rushes out on to the level below. So much for the jump itself.

Make the descent toward the "take-off" with body erect and well balanced, leaning slightly forward and with skis close together. As you near the jump, assume a crouching position such that your hands will come down by your ankles. Even in this position, remember the watchword "Lean Forward" and keep the weight on the balls of the feet. Jumping has been aptly described as an unrolling process. Just in time, but not too soon, commence this unrolling or spring upward, so that it will be finished with your body erect and under good control, just at the instant the part of the skis under your feet reaches the very edge of the jump.

Some have found it better not to crouch until the last possible moment. Stand erect and well-balanced until within a few feet of the edge, then drop into the crouching position and spring up again vigorously almost in the same motion, just as the brink is reached. Delaying this dropping-down to the last moment prevents the jumper from making the spring too soon, which is a common fault. On the other hand, it compels him to spring up again snappily or the spring will be finished in the air, which is apt to be disastrous. The benefit of this snappy up-spring is shown in the increased power and stability of the jump.

Remember to lean forward, and while you are in the air try to lean forward even more. He will jump farthest who can time his spring the most accurately and make it the most vigorously. Keep your nerve and don't be discouraged if you fall. Don't forget "Il faut de l'audace et encore de l'audace, et toujours de l'audace." Remember ski-jumping is just like everything else really worth while, it only comes after good hard work and consistent. practice. "Keep at

A Telemark Swing

it" is perhaps the best advice of all. If you do this, you will be sure to make good.

TELEMARK AND CHRISTIANA SWINGS

These beautiful turns alone would class skiing as a great sport, are very useful "en tour," and should be mastered as soon as possible.

To start the Telemark swing, say to the right, push the left ski forward until the middle of the forward ski comes opposite the point of the ski in back. The weight should now be almost wholly on the forward foot and the right knee should be bent so as almost to touch the fore part of the blade of the ski. This "Telemark Knee" position is the most important preparation; you should be so balanced that you can rise and fall with an elastic spring.

Now turn the point of the left ski rather vigorously to the right, and at the same time lean sharply to the right and a little forward. You will find yourself coming around with a graceful swing. Make these movements with a certain dash and abandon—the turn is something you must not be too methodical about. Do not rise too soon after coming around, as the swing takes some time to finish. The ski must be long enough so that the point of the back ski will not slip past the front foot and cross behind it. The turn to the left is made in just the same way with all motions reversed. The advanced leg is always on the "outside" of the swing. That is, if you want to make a swing to the left, you advance your right leg, and vice versa. The Telemark is at its best in deep snow and is very useful for cross-country. work.

The Christiana is a shorter, quicker turn, and is more like "slewing" around. If a turn to the right is desired, the right foot is advanced, but only a few inches ahead of the other. It is necessary to effect this turn by a vigorous twisting of the body. Twist the body as if you were attempting to sit down in a chair at your left side without bending your knees. You must, however, lean to the right when the swing is started. You will find yourself coming around with a rush. If care is not taken the tails of the skis will cross each other in back. In the Christiana, the weight is about equally divided on both skis, whereas in the Telemark, it is placed almost wholly on the advanced foot.

All swings should be drawn—not jerked. Whereas the curve is above all useful and reliable, there is no reason why it shouldn't be executed in a graceful manner.

In comparing the swings, Rickmers says:—"The Christiana is brisk, short, quick; it is most effective and efficient on a steep slope. The long, stately swoop of the Telemark, with the body low down on the ground

"Tracks" Note Herring-boning on Right

has a peculiar aesthetic fascination of its own. Seen from a good view point above, it shows a black dot traversed by the slender arrow of extended ski.

The Christiana, with body at full length, and ski but little extended, rushes and swerves against the steep side of the hill, like a stout craft on a rapid river. The Telemark, like a long, slender skiff with a short man, glides majestically through a wide expanse."

Of stemming, snow-ploughing, herring-boning and the many other departments of skiing, there is no room

Leaving the "Take-Off"

here in which to speak. These all simply go to show how diversified are its elements and how really worth while skiing is. Following are a few of the terms used in the sport.

To dart—to descend with parallel ski in a narrow spoor.

To curve—to make short circular swoops.

To stem—to regulate speed by forming a half snow-plough with the ski.

To swing—to swish around at full speed.

The "saats"—the term applied to the straightening up, or "unrolling" process used in jumping.

Herring-boning—climbing steep slopes by means of edging the skis and straddling the points apart until they nearly form a right angle with each other. The tails are lifted over each other at each step.

Side-stepping—climbing up hill by stepping sidewise, leaving tracks resembling a stairway.

The kick-turn—a very useful means of turning around on the spot, accomplished with three motions.

The approach—that part of the course above the jump.

The "take-off"—the edge of the jump itself.

The "alighting ground"—the steep slope on which the jumpers land.

The "outrun"—the level stretch at the foot of the hill on which the jumpers check their speed.

A Song of the Ski

[FROM THE YEAR BOOK OF THE SKI CLUB OF GREAT BRITAIN.]

A King, I ween, it must have been,
  All in the North Countree.
Who freed his folks from the Snow-fiend's yoke
  By teaching the use of the Ski.

'Tis said, one day, as asleep he lay,
  In a vision he did see,
How men might glide down the mountain side,
  As ships glide over the sea.

Then he up and laughed, "I will make a raft
  A raft for each foot;" quoth he;
"For, methinks, they should go o'er the billowy snow,
  As they go o'er the billowy sea."

So an ash tree sound he felled to the ground
  All in the North Countree,
And cleft it in twain, with a straight running grain,
  To fashion the faery Ski.

Two supple strips with upturned tips
  He carved from the river tree
And with leathern thong to his ankles strong
  He lashed the new born Ski.

'Twas rapture supreme, passing vision or dream,
  No longer he sank to the knee,
But with curve, dip and swing, like a bird on the wing,
  He sped o'er the snow on his Ski.

Then o'er hill and dale with an even trail,
  He fared through the North Countree,
And he cried with delight as he skimmed from the height
  "Hurrah! for the fleeting Ski."

And thus the sport to the world was taught,
  All in the North Countree;
And the snow no more keeps folk within door,
  For they all fare forth on their Ski.

AN AUTHORITY ABROAD GIVES US THE FOLLOWING
DESCRIPTION OF THE WAY IN WHICH SKIING HAS
SPREAD OVER EUROPE

In tracing the development of the sport, we discover that although the ski has been used as a means of locomotion from time immemorial in Scandinavia, it is only since the '70's that the development of ski-running as a sport can be traced. During recent years, it has spread rapidly over the rest of Europe, indeed beyond its limits. Sweden, Austria and Germany were among the first countries to come under the spell of the new sport. The Swiss soon became keen enthusiasts; France and Italy, impressed like other Continental nations with the utility of the ski for military purposes, have paid special attention to this branch of the pursuit; Hungarian and Polish ski clubs flourish in the High Tatra district; Montenegro, Albania and Turkey were invaded by skis three years ago; we read of ski-running in Spain; rumor has it that a club has been formed in Servia; in fact there is hardly a country in Europe where a beginning has not been made.

It is also remarkable how this snow sport of the north has steadily pushed its way southward regardless almost of latitude, and has even gained a footing beneath the rays of the African sun. For several years past it has flourished in Algeria, and it will not be long before we shall hear of it in the mountains of Morocco.

Why ski-running should have spread over the world just when it did, it is difficult to say. Probably an impetus was given by the publication of Dr. Nansen's classical work, "The First Crossing of Greenland," which served to bring to the notice of a wide public the great utility of the ski. Probably the recent successful explorer of the South Pole, Amundsen, could add much valuable testimony as to how he gained the goal on ski.

In our own country ski clubs are flourishing all through the middle west, and successful tournaments are held each year at Duluth, Minn., Ishpeming, Mich., Ashland and Coleraine, Wis., Ironwood, Mich., and many other places.   In Canada we find a very flourishing organization in the Montreal Ski Club, which has held many successful jumping competitions and is now contemplating the building of a club house in the wonderful Laurentian hills.

FROM OUR NEIGHBOR, THE MONTREAL SKI CLUB

The following account kindly sent in by Mr. James Kerr of the Montreal Ski Club shows how skiing, as a sport, first made its appearance in Canada, and the wonderful progress that has since been made.—*Ed*.

It is uncertain who first used skis in Montreal; as far as it may be ascertained they made their appearance in this vicinity about 1881. Apparently they were of the Lapland type, about twelve feet long and narrow. It was understood at that time that they were really a form of snowskate to be used with the same motion, and as such did not appeal to local athletes. About 1900, however, the shorter skis came in and these provided the new sport of sliding and cross-country running for which Mount Royal provided ideal conditions. Some primitive jumps were made from time to time and the possibilities of the sport became better recognized. Therefore when a meeting was called of those interested in the formation of a club, a hearty response was shown and the result was the organizing of the Montreal Ski Club.

A Quintet of Devotees from the Montreal Ski Club

The objects of the club were to be the holding of jumping competitions, cross-country running and the looking after the interests of skiers in general. The work since done in this direction has shown very satisfactory results. Whereas in 1904 there were probably only about two hundred pairs of skis in use in Montreal, there are now, as far as may be estimated, much over *ten thousand.*

The first fixture of the club was a Jumping Competition held in February, 1904, at which the competitors were Norwegians, resident in the city. It was a novelty to the thousands who viewed it and great enthusiasm was shown in this spectacular new sport. A short time after this, a second competition was held, at which some entries of club members showed that local men could be counted upon to give a good account of themselves in the future. This made the club officers decide to make the competitions open, and not to divide them into Norwegian and Canadian classes as at first. The home men have always been quite willing to compete on equal terms, even if unable to get first honors as often as might be desired, and this spirit is noticeably evident in skiing. So many of our competitive sports have become tinged with professionalism that the amateurism of skiing places it in the highest rank.

Having been fortunate in getting without charge the use of grounds for the Jumps, spectators were invited to view the competitions as guests of the club. Recently, increasing expenditures for attendants and care of the Jumps made it advisable to charge a small admission fee for the championships. The Junior event and the Saturday weekly club competitions, however, are open to the public, and thousands view them and enjoy the entertainment they afford.

On many occasions noted guests have attended these fixtures, including the Governors of Canada and foreign visitors, the banner attendance being when Earl Grey and his party were present, when over ten thousand spectators were treated to a splendid exhibition.

While jumping, which is the spectacular form of skiing, has brought the club more prominently before the public eye, the cross-country running has provided a social sport to the larger number of members. Mount Royal has given splendid opportunity for this right at home, and the sight of members so enjoying themselves has given an incentive to outsiders to take up the sport. In fact snowshoeing, which for years was looked upon as particularly a Montreal sport, has had to take second place in the list of Canadian Snow Sports. Particularly is this noticeable in the younger generations, and boys and girls are as enthusiastic as their elders. Hundreds of ladies also take part, and very creditably too.

With the Laurentian Mountains a little over an hour's run up north it is possible to enjoy winter scenery that so compares with that of Europe that this part of Canada is spoken of as the Switzerland of Canada.

The Ski Club annual fixtures include three week-end trips to the mountains, one to Shawbridge at the foothills, and two to Ste Agathe des Monts, sixty-five miles from Montreal. The C. P. R. provide for these a private car which is attached to the train leaving Place Viger Station at 1.30 P.M. Saturday, and returns Sunday night.

On one of these trips the officers entertain, and this event includes a concert in aid of local benevolences of Ste Agathe, followed by supper. The following day a free for all cross-country race is, for the members, one of the most interesting fixtures of the season. As the club has many local entertainers in its membership, the concerts are always to a full house, and very welcome sums have been realized for the associations that benefit.

These trips have done much to promote the social side of the sport, and, needless to say, accommodation is always taxed to the utmost.

The experience in Montreal has proven the benefit of having an organized club to promote the general welfare.

In Eastern Canada, Toronto, Ottawa, Quebec, Three Rivers, Sherbrooke and Grand Mere now have clubs and members from these take part in the events of each other. Each season sees clubs in new districts, and it may be a likely possibility that in the near future entries from European countries will add to the present interest of the Canadian Championships.

The representative list of past officers denotes the high position skiing takes in Eastern Canada, and from both officers and members a hearty welcome is assured to visitors of other countries who may visit Montreal during the winter season, either for competitions or for the mountain trips.

Mr. Wendel L. Paul, Honorary Secretary-Treasurer of the above Club, has signified his intention of accompanying the Outing Club this winter on its annual trip to the White Mountains. To Mr. Paul, and to all others of the fraternity of outdoor life, the Outing Club extends a warm welcome. Mr. Paul has had much experience on ski tours in Switzerland and on looking for a new field in this country, he stated that he wished to try this trip.—*Ed*.

CRAMMER'S LIST

Suggestions for Skiing

General

Are bindings and outfit in order?
Try to understand each position.
Practice slowly with a little methodical exaggeration.
Study first in a still position.
First take separate positions, then combine.
Change about right and left, do not become one-sided.   Change
your ground frequently.

What is Wrong?

If unsuccessful, ask yourself:—
Is the position correct (ski, body, etc.)?
Are the skis too short or too long?
Does the binding fit properly?
Is the snow sticky?   Are the skis too slippery?
Is the slope of snow favorable to this particular movement?
Is the exercise in question possible or necessary under these
conditions?
Am I tired or handicapped by clothing in any way?

MEMORANDA FOR TRIPS

Start early.
Has nothing been forgotten?
Count the members of the party.
Go slowly; regulate pace suitable to weakest member.
Keep together.
Lunch before getting into the wind; eat not too late.
Get things done (eating, repairs, etc.,) while the sun shines or
while there is an easy opportunity.
Always keep your eyes open and think.
Always expect change of weather, nightfall.
The snow over streams is often hollow.
When in difficulties, think, do not hurry, do not allow relaxa-
tion among the members of the party.
If lost, mark the spot and reason out; when did we leave the
proper route, and did we turn right or left?   Which is the
right general direction?   Do not go in a circle, but keep
straight by looking back on track.
Ask for help when in trouble; say when you are tired, ill or
threatened with frost-bite.
Take off ski when not feeling safe.
Turn back before it is too late.

One of the Series of Ski-Jumping Tournaments

*GOOD BOOKS AND ANNUALS TO GET TOWARD A SKI LIBRARY:

"The Skisport" Year Book of the National Association.
"The Ski-Runner," by E. C. Richardson.
"With Ski in Norway and Lapland," by J. H. W. Fulton.
"The Year Book of the Ski Club of Great Britain."
"Winter Sports Review," Edited by E. C. Richardson.
"Ski-Chronik"—Jahrbuch des Mitteleuropaischen Ski Verbandes.
"Ski"—Jahrbuch des Schweiz Ski-Verbandes.
"Skilobning," af Fritz Huitfeldt.
The Alpine Ski Club Annual.
"Aarbog"—Year Book of the Norwegian Association.
"Der Schi," by Henry Hoek.

---

*Even if the books are written in a language you do not understand, the illustrations alone are worth the cost.

Snowshoe Suggestions.

This brief sketch will attempt to answer the simplest questions of the beginner on snowshoes.

The first question is, "What shoes shall I buy?" There are several distinct types of shoes. The beginner should take especial care not to yield to the temptation of buying an extreme size or shape which may give him more trouble than pleasure.

The so-called Indian racer is the extremely long,

Single File

narrow shoe built for high speed in deep snow. For the ordinary tramper on the New Hampshire hills, it is far too long, especially when it is a question of negotiating sheep-wire fences, ditches, thickets, and brush-piles.

The Bear Paw is a short, broad shoe largely used by trappers because of ease of manipulation in the woods, allowing the possibility of quick, short turns. It is little used for work in the open country but is sometimes used for mountain-climbing.

The shoe most commonly used in New Hampshire measures twelve or fourteen inches across and from forty-two to forty-eight inches in length. This type has proved the most satisfactory combination for use in the open country, on hills, and in the woods.

There are numerous points to be considered in selecting the shoe:

1. See that the frame is clean, clear-grained, and strong, especially where the cross-bars are inserted. At the same time the frame should be light.

2. Get a good quality of gut, with few knots, strung not too close, in order that fine snow may easily be sifted off when the foot is raised.

3. Don't have the toe bent very much. Some people prefer absolutely flat points, but a very slight curve helps to avoid tripping. Some snowshoers prefer a shoe without webbing in the toe, as less likely to trip, but in such a shoe there is just that much less supporting power, noticeable especially in deep, soft snow or on a down-hill slope.

4. Be sure that the shoe balances well on your foot. The greater part of the weight should be behind the toe fastening, so that in running, the tail will drag along the ground. If the weight is too evenly distributed, the toes will dip into the snow, with disastrous results.

5. Be sure that the shoes are narrow enough so that you can walk without spreading the feet unnaturally. The attempt to use a shoe too broad to fit the natural stride is very fatiguing.

A word as to bindings: if you get patent toe clips, the critical place is where they join the shoe. If this joint is made with a single small strip of rawhide or leather,

be sure that it is firmly tied, and is *shrunk* so that it cannot stretch and allow play—for play in a snowshoe
harness means *blisters*. Some people use coarse copper
wire to make this joint, winding it a number of times.
This gives a semi-flexible joint with almost no stretch,
and if carefully put on, will not injure the gut of the shoe.

One of the most satisfactory types of harness, however, is that in which a single strap runs through the
toe-cap, down into the snowshoe, back through the
toe-cap, and fastens behind the heel. Every time the

A Spill

heel strap is tightened, the joint under the toe is tightened automatically. A very convenient addition to this
harness is a small strip of leather or raw-hide sewed low
on the heel of boot or moccasin through which the heel
strap may be passed and securely held in place. There
will be no trouble from ankle blisters if the strap is low
enough on the heel.

For footgear, be sure to have it large, warm, and
above all, comfortable. Heel-less rubber shoes with
leather tops are often used. Ordinary high-buckle over-

Up the Mt. Washington Carriage Road

A. M. C. Shelter

shoes are fairly satisfactory if worn over warm boots. Moccasins are the regulation outfit. One can wear several pairs of woolen socks inside them, or better still, an inner moccasin of sheep-skin with the wool on; this gives a soft, warm pad which keeps the foot comfortable and free from blisters or chafing. Heavy lumbermen's leggings are good to wear with moccasins. It is essential to have knee-high leggings of some sort, as the snowshoes kick up the snow about knee-high behind each leg.   D. E. ADAMS.

FIRE BUILDING OUT-OF-DOORS

A few hints on fire building, clothing, cooking and sleeping out in the winter, from knowledge gained by the students from actual experiences of trips spent in the woods, may be of some assistance to those who wish to go and do likewise.—*Ed.*

The prime requisite in fire building is naturally dry wood. For material to start the fire there is nothing better than birch bark, which will burn even when wet. In order to secure fine dry wood one needs only to break off the lower dead branches of soft wood trees, especially balsam and spruce. The inside of dead logs is also dry, if they have not decayed to the punky stage.

The dry wood having been obtained, one needs only to start the fire with the birch bark and fine dry wood, then piling on the larger wood in such a way that there is plenty of chance for the air to circulate, entering at the bottom and passing out at the top of the pile. Thus a draft is created which causes the fire to burn briskly. Great care must be taken not to smother the flames by attempting to pile on too much wood.

Cooking Out-of-doors

The preceding article tells one how to get the fire started. After one sees that the fire is well under way he can suspend the pots or kettles over the flames by running a stout green stick through the handles, and resting the stick in two forked limbs driven into the ground on each side of the fire. In order to fry or broil any meat or fish over the fire one should wait until the flames have died down somewhat and there is a steady hot glow from the embers. Potatoes also can be easily baked in the coals.

In frying food, one should have only enough grease in the pan to prevent the food from catching and burning, otherwise the grease will cause the article to be soggy and heavy.

Sleeping Out in Winter

In order to do this, one should, if possible, choose his site in some evergreen growth, so as to be protected from the wind. A large rubber or waterproof blanket should be laid on the boughs, which have been scattered over the snow where one intends to sleep. If it is a very cold night one should select a site where a slanting ledge would reflect the heat from the fire, built close under it. The other blankets should be of wool, as for its weight wool is the warmest covering of all. A sleeping bag is a very handy thing in the winter. This has its waterproof cover, which makes the bag nearly airtight, and therefore much warmer.

A number of Outing Club parties have slept overnight in the snow even when the thermometer was below zero, and have reported that they slept well and were comfortable during the night.   C. E. S.

CLOTHING

The matter of clothing to be used on skiing or snow-shoeing trips is of very great importance and should always be given careful consideration before starting out, especially if the expedition is to be a long one. Do not be afraid to wear old clothes. It is best to sacrifice appearance for the sake of warmth and service.

On ordinary trips on the lower levels the tendency at first is to wear too much rather than too little clothing. Remember that cold, in a way, is a comparative

Where Old Clothes come in Handy

quantity. To a person coming out from a hot room with the body functioning imperfectly, the weather may seem cold. To that same person, when the blood begins to circulate vigorously and his lungs are being filled to their full capacity, his ability to measure cold is, to a degree, lost. It is then that the cold and the keen air are welcome and much clothing is not needed. In the dry air at Hanover, it is entirely possible to start out some fairly warm, still afternoon and before returning have the thermometer drop 30 degrees or 40 degrees without this being appreciably felt.

If, however, it is to be a mountain-climbing trip, plenty of clothing should always be carried, for, no matter what the weather, the extra garments will all be needed when the wind begins to get in its sweep above the timber-line. Since climbing is hot work even in very severe weather, it is best to wear fairly light under-clothing and rely for the needed warmth on outer garments, which can be carried on the way up and put on when the chill begins to strike in.

For the outer garment a coat which is as nearly wind-proof as possible should be worn, and it should be made to button close around the neck and wrists in order to keep out the snow. It should also have a smooth surface; otherwise the snow will cling to it and melt. For this reason a sweater is very unsatisfactory and should never be worn as an outer garment, although sweaters are excellent to use as extra garments under the outer coat.

Socks are a very important item and heavy woolen ones are the best. At least two pairs should be worn. The extra room these will take up should be borne in mind when purchasing boots or moccasins. Extra pairs should also be taken along, because no matter how waterproof the boot, the stockings cannot be kept dry, owing to the perspiration.

Gloves and headgear are also important and should be selected with care. Mittens are better than gloves as they are warm even when wet. It is best to take an extra pair of these also along as it is impossible to keep them dry on long trips.

A big heavy toque makes an excellent headgear, but

" All Hands Around." Hermit Lake Camp. 1912

" Back to College"

two should be taken along, as in strong winds one is not sufficient. Combination storm caps, which turn down, forming a hood and face mask, are also very good.

J. Y. C.

(The following items of camp outfitting given us by W. Lee White may serve to help some prospective camper.)

A very satisfactory addition to the provisions for a camping-out trip is a supply of the "Dehydro" fruits and vegetables sold by Montgomery & Ward. They *are not* ordinary dried fruits, but the water is extracted by a special patented process, leaving them unbelievably light and convenient. To prepare, you simply boil according to directions; or, if you desire to use them in some other way, by soaking a few hours in water you make fresh vegetables and fruits of them. They seem exactly as delicious as the fresh article and make camping a much more convenient proposition. One can each of "Dehydro" parsley, onion and celery will last for several weeks as seasonings, and, with erbswurst and beef tablets for a base, offer a possibility for a very delicious soup. I recommend these inexpensive "Dehydro" goods, without qualification, to all out-of-doors. One of our tents is also worthy of mention. It is 7 x 7 x 7; weighs but five and one half pounds; is entirely waterproof, and will accommodate two persons and their duffel comfortably in permanent camp or three for overnight stops. Besides its other qualifications, the tent needs but four stakes and no pole, provided there is a nearly overhead branch. It is put on the market by The George Tent Co., St. Paul, Minn.

D. O. C. Notes
Personal and Otherwise
A Tribute of the Snowpath

THE third season found the Outing Club in a prosperous condition. Whether or not, however, the Club should go ahead or backward depended in a great measure on the ability and interest of its new president. That the Club passed the most prosperous year of its existence is due to the unfailing energy and zeal of that ardent lover of the out-of-doors, W. Lee White.

It was his enthusiasm and optimism that made the Club take the leap forward that it did during the season of 1911-1912. Many cross-country trips were taken; the Winter Carnival was a greater success than ever before; and the Club came out ahead financially.

Those of us who have been off with Lee on the trail are only too glad to pay tribute to his sportsmanship and his knowledge of the woods. When he swings into his long lope on snowshoes, there are but few who can follow his pace. Even downhill on skis, I have tried in vain to "shake" him. Lee is "some" cook, too. Within half an hour of the time that camp is made, Lee will have a real live camp all built. A crane has been built on which is steaming a pot of coffee, and underneath the bacon is frizzling. At one side, he has built a table of small logs, now all set, and at the cry of "Supper ready," we all sit down to partake of his handiwork.

The past summer, Lee was head cook for a geology expedition, led by Prof. J. W. Goldthwaite, which had its camp only a few hundred yards from Hermit Lake near Tuckerman's Ravine. Many valuable discoveries were made by Professor Goldthwaite on the traces of glaciers in the White Mountains and his report ought to be most interesting. Although the expedition lasted five weeks, no complaint was made of lack of variety of the food.

W. Lee White , President 1911-1912

During the summer, I had the good fortune to visit the camp of this expedition. Descending from Mt. Washington, through Tuckerman's Ravine, following the line of "The Fall of a Thousand Cascades," in a short hour I dropped some two thousand five hundred feet in altitude and passed through some of the grandest scenery it has ever been my good fortune to enjoy.

At the bottom of the ravine, the last traces of the famous "Snow Arch" were still visible and I made snow-balls from it—this on the 7th of August. Continuing on down the trail, which in many instances follows the bed of the brook, I came to the path which leads to Hermit Lake. It was with pleasure that I noticed a small arrow shaped sign on which I read "Dartmouth Geology Camp," and following the path through an unbroken wilderness, I soon burst on the camp itself. It was an ideal situation amid a mass of evergreens with the mountain brook roaring by, only a few feet away.

Lee soon had a bountiful supper awaiting us and never have I had anything which tasted better. After listening to the accounts of the day's happenings by Professor Goldthwaite, we turned in. It had been a strenuous day for me and it was with a feeling of relief that I crawled into the sleeping bag awaiting me. The next morning, we awoke to hear the rain pattering on the tent, and after breakfast it was with regret that I took up the trail again and said good-bye to the camp which had been so hospitable to me.

Lee hails from Stamford, Conn. This fall he enters the Law School of Yale University and it is with a hearty appreciation of what he has done for the Club that his fellow members of the D. O. C. wish him all kinds of success in his new studies.

A New Helmsman

The President of the Club is again a ski man. The plans of the policies for the season of 1912-1913 lie in the hands of Carl E. Shumway of Melrose, Mass., who perhaps more than any other member of the Club has been an exponent of cross-country ski-running. In the number of miles travelled on regulation trips, his total was well up in the front rank last season, and in addition, he took many long personal trips which were not scheduled.

On his first cross-country trips "Shum" used snow-shoes as much as he did skis; in fact, on the ascent of Mt. Washington, on the first White Mountain trip, he in-

Carl E. Shumway

sisted on using snowshoes in spite of any arguments to the contrary. Now, however, he is a full-fledged ski enthusiast and I doubt if you could get him to put on a pair of snowshoes. Last winter, he went up Mt. Washington on skis and made the four mile descent from the Half Way house in eighteen minutes, in contrast to his time of an hour and a half on snowshoes of the year before.

One of the first long ski tours by any member of the Club was undertaken last year, when accompanied by

G. L. Foster, "Shum" went on a five-day cross-country trip over the hills of New Hampshire which before its completion provided many experiences and led him to the top of Mt. Moosilauke and back.

Last summer he spent his vacation managing the Stage Office on the top of Mt. Washington, and the year before, he spent the summer with his father camping out in Canada, so he is well acquainted with the woods. In addition to being an ardent lover of out-door sports, he is a thinker and a good executive, and under his guidance the Club should pass through a very prosperous year.

Sportsmanship of the Race

It was during the cross-country ski-race of 1911. The finish of the struggle was nearing. Through ignorance of the course, having never been around it before, the leader in the race, when leading by some hundred yards mistook one of the cross-country snowshoe flags for a ski-flag, got off the course and found himself wallowing in the deep snow. Meanwhile, the second man was gaining on him two feet to his one. The man behind had only to keep still and the race would undoubtedly have been his. Instead of that, he called out, "Say, that's not the right way," then gave him the right instructions how to reach the beaten path and thus the leader was able to come in a few yards ahead. How many men would have spoken when silence meant victory?

The man was Arthur T. Cobb, '12, and he was one of a few. Champion ski-jumper of the college in 1911 and 1912, he has been our champion on many a cross-country trip and was always to the front and always reliable.

"Ty" is married now, being one of the first of the Outing Clubbers to give up the single life. He was studying in the medical school, but this new event in his life caused him to give up medicine. He now has a position with Filene's in Boston, and in his last letter

A. T. Cobb

he reported that he was very pleasantly situated. Good luck, "Ty."

FUND STARTED FOR BUILDING CABINS.

A fund has been started with which to continue the work of building the chain of cabins. The first cabin is situated at the base of Moose Mountain. The second one is to be built on Sugar Hill, west of Holt's Ledge, where a scouting party has made investigations and has reported the finding of a favorable location and the all necessary supply of water.

The proceeds realized from the sale of this book are all going toward the above fund, so, members and friends of the Club, buy a book for yourselves and send some to your friends and thus help the good work along.

RED TRAILS.

A characteristic expression of Outing life, a relic brought down to us from olden days and symbolical of the time when Samuel Ocom and his Indian companions used to roam these same hills, will be the Outing Club trails. These will be indicated by splotches of red or yellow paint placed at intervals above the snow line on trees or other available landmarks. The first trail should be made to the cabin on Moose Mountain. If a trail is made with care, it is oftentimes possible to include many little spots of beauty which would otherwise be passed unnoticed and to avoid difficult places which would cause trouble. This work will place permanent evidences of the Club's existence on the surrounding country. It is hoped that those who follow the trails will become interested in and help to support the Club.

PRIZE FOR GREATEST MILEAGE.

To arouse still more interest in the cross-country trips, the benefits of which so many men availed themselves last year, the Club is contemplating this season the offering of a prize to that member who at the end of the winter has gone the greatest number of miles on regulation trips. The possibility of awarding insignia for results accomplished is likewise being discussed.

In Mid-Air

JUMPING HILL IMPROVED.
DUAL SKI-JUMPING COMPETITION POSSIBLE

The jump was enlarged and improved the past fall in preparation for the winter's contests. It is hoped that the course will be in such good condition that a record of 70 feet or over will be hung up this year. By moving the jump to the right a more nearly straightaway course has been obtained. This, together with grading above the jump so as to make the approach smooth, and filling in below to make the alighting ground steeper, has made a great improvement. The slide faces nearly North, which is ideal.

The beautiful amphitheatre formed by the converging slopes enables a large number of spectators to see the contests to advantage. The natural beauty of this sheltered spot, with the stately pines at the foot and the wooded slopes on either side, makes the Vale of Tempe an ideal place at which to hold the ski-jumping competitions. It is hoped that each year the length of the record jump, engraved on the championship cup, will grow longer and longer, until Dartmouth can send out men able to compete with the best ski-jumpers in the land.

Dartmouth would very much like to arrange a dual Winter Meet with some other college, and hereby extends an invitation to any college interested in this matter to correspond with the secretary of the Outing Club.

A dual Ski-Jumping Competition with another college would be very interesting. The natural excitement of the sport coupled with the zeal of Intercollegiate competition would produce a spectacle hard to equal. A dual meet with either of our Canadian neighbors, McGill or Toronto would be welcome.

TRAIL BLAZED TO PIERMONT MOUNTAIN

Prof. C. D. Adams and his two sons, while camping on Armington Pond this summer, blazed a new trail to the summit of Piermont Mountain (2,400), running a line due northwest from the southern extremity of the pond. The trail was clearly spotted, and the brush sufficiently cleared to make the ascent easy. Piermont Mountain lies in a direct line between Piermont station on the river, and Glencliff, the base station for Moosilauke, on the White Mountains division. The mountain rises immediately above and west of the Tarleton ponds, famous for the new Lake Tarleton Club, and affords a splendid view of Moosilauke, Cube, the Green Mountains, and the beautiful river country in all directions.

CLUBHOUSE ON MOOSE MOUNTAIN

During the fall, several parties have visited the Moose Mountain cabin. This trip seems to be the favorite "rendezvous" of "Outing Clubbers," and with its ideal situation, this should be the real central gathering place of the D. O. C. A larger club house of a plain design is planned to be built there, which will accommodate two dozen or more for overnight visits.

A NEW TRAIL PLANNED

A project now in mind is to blaze a trail to the highest peak of the Dartmouth Range in the White Mountains, and thus by putting visible evidences of the activities of the Club on the range which bears the name of the college to call the attention of the outside world to its work. This idea came from President Shumway. A few members of the Club could put in a very enjoyable week on the work during next summer. Volunteers wanted!

EXPEDITION TO THE DARTMOUTH GRANT

Another possibility not as yet taken advantage of is to send each year a scouting party to that vast tract of wilderness in Northern New Hampshire known as the

Our Genial Friend, Dr. Licklider

Dartmouth Grant. The college should know this country more intimately and the Outing Club could well serve as the pioneer in spreading information as to this interesting section. This trip should appeal to hunters, for it is a paradise there for game, and a hunting lodge is not at all an impossibility.

A TRIBUTE TO THE SKI

From the successful Antarctic explorer we have the following "I attribute my success to my splendid comrades and to the magnificent work of the dogs, and next to them TO OUR SKIS, and to the splendid condition of the dogs on landing in the Antarctic."

AMUNDSEN.

DISTRESS SIGNALS

The Club has under consideration the establishment of some standard signal of distress. It is difficult to over-emphasize the importance of this step.

The distress signals of the Swiss Alpine Club are as follows:—

OPTICAL SIGNALS

By day — Wave six times a minute, describing a semi-circle away from the sun, any object whatsoever, preferably a rag or garment, tied to a stick, then pause a minute and repeat.

By night—Display a light (lantern, fire, etc.) six times a minute. Pause a minute and repeat.

ACOUSTIC SIGNALS

Repeat a short shrill cry, or shoot a gun six times a minute, then pause a minute and repeat.

THE REPLY TO A SIGNAL OF DISTRESS

is given by means of an optical or acoustic signal repeated three (3) times a minute and followed by a minute's pause.

Tuckerman's Ravine. Here the Snow Drifts Reach a Depth of 90 Feet or More. Height of Headwall and Depth of Snow May be Indicated by a Comparison with the Figures of the Two Men which Appear as Dots in the Center

Getting Ready to Start

The Dartmouth Outing Club is intending to correspond with the Appalachian Mountain Climbing Club and other clubs interested, and is hoping to agree with them on some such standard signals as the ones given above.

You may scarcely ever wish to give this signal, but when you do,————!

CO-OPERATION OF PHYSICAL CULTURE DEPARTMENT.

POSSIBILITIES FOR FOOTBALL TRAINING.

The physical culture director of the college, Dr. John W. Bowler, has always been a staunch friend of the Outing Club and has expressed himself in sympathy with its work. During the present season, he has occasionally excused from the gymnasium classes those Freshmen who wished to take advantage of the Outing Club trips. Certain it is that anyone who makes the most of the splendid gymnasium equipment and the training under Dr. Bowler and who couples this with much outdoor exercise and follows this schedule conscientiously through the four years of his college life, will emerge with a wonderfully improved physique and with improved qualifications for the needs of later life.

If the football men would enter vigorously into the winter sports activities instead of hibernating after the football season is over, as is sometimes the case, it would keep them in good condition through the winter and would give them a foundation of vitality and endurance that would put the team one step nearer winning the important games the next fall. To the Freshmen, to the football men, to all,—Hanover winter life offers a wealth of opportunity. Do not let it pass.

Trails from the Campus

THE following outlines have been prepared for the purpose of putting in concrete and condensed form the possibilities of outdoor life in and around Hanover. They are arranged in the order of distance to be covered and time consumed, so that anyone, having a few hours, or an afternoon, at his disposal, may select for himself, with due knowledge and without the necessity for inquiry, a trip to suit his desires. If a longer trip or mountain climb is preferred, that also can be found correspondingly, and the approximate time of trains has been given. The time of trains should always be looked up, however, before starting on a trip.

In Corbin Park Game Preserve

These trips have all been personally gone over, and are, as nearly as possible, accurate; but it is advised that a map be taken along, especially on the longer trips. When there is any doubt as to the road, questions should be asked. In this connection, it may be said that the Officers of the Dartmouth Outing Club are always glad to confer with anyone regarding trips, and will appreciate any information regarding mistakes in these trails, or concerning new trails which may be added.

The trails, as a rule, follow the roads, and can therefore be used for driving or sleighing, but in the winter, when on skis or snowshoes, or even in the summer when walking, it is often better to leave the prescribed trail and "strike out" across the fields or through the woods, in which case a map is necessary unless the country is known. Many variations and combinations can also be made with the aid of a map, or if one is familiar with the surroundings, this being especially true in winter, when the river and ponds can be crossed on the ice.

1. ROPE FERRY AND GOLF LINKS.

Distance 3 miles
Time 1 hour

North on Main Street past Hospital to river at the "first island" and old Rope Ferry. Left along path by the river, across Golf Links to Hospital.

2. THE VALE OF TEMPE

Distance 3 miles
Time 1 hour

Through College Park to northeast corner; down Lyme road or across fields to the Vale. Follow path along the stream about half a mile to the river. Turn to left by the old Rope Ferry and return via the Golf Links or road (No. 1). This is the beautiful and famous Vale of Tempe, where Daniel Webster is said to have gone to practice his speeches.

3. VELVET ROCKS.

Distance 3 miles
Time 1½ hours

East on Wheelock Street to stone house on hill. Take trail to right by big elm tree to top of Velvet Rocks, where a fine view is obtained. Return same way or down north side to road.

4. BALCH HILL AND RESERVOIR.

Distance 4 miles
Time 1½ hours

East on Wheelock Street up Balch Hill. Left at Fork to Reservoir, or, left by house at top of hill, across the fields to the top of the knoll, where a fine view is obtained, and down the northeast side to the Reservoir. Left at Reservoir, down valley to the Lyme road and south to Hanover.

5. WILDER.

Distance 5 miles
Time 2 hours

South on Main Street, continuing on State road. About two miles down take right hand road to Wilder, crossing the river by bridge above dam and paper mills, (a beautiful sight is seen here, especially in the winter.) Return by R.R. or straight through Wilder and the right hand road to the Hartford road. North, taking right at fork down hill to Norwich Station and Hanover.

6. PINEO HILL.

Distance 7 miles
Time 3 hours

No. 4 or Lyme Road to Reservoir. (By Lyme Road take first right about 1 mile beyond corner of College Park.) East on road north of Reservoir, and left at cross-roads (dotted on map). Top of hill is left of road about one-half mile from cross-roads. An excellent view is obtained from the top, about 200 yards above the road. Return same way or by same road north to Lyme road and thence to Hanover.

7. Bragg School and Dothan.

Distance 9 miles
Time 3½ hours

Cross to Norwich Station. Straight over R.R. and right, up hill to Norwich. Left at Newton Inn, right about one block down, and left at cross-roads, up Bragg Brook to schoolhouse. Left past farm house to fork, left to Dothan and Hartford road. North, taking right at fork down hill to Norwich station and Hanover.

8. White River Junction.

Distance 10 miles
Time 3 hours

South on Main Street to West Lebanon. Cross river to Junction and return by R.R. or road to Wilder and thence to Hanover, either way (see No. 5).

9. Pompanoosuc.

Distance 10 miles
Time 3 hours

Cross to Norwich Station. North by R.R., or River Road to Pompanoosuc. Return same way, or via Tilden Hill.

10. Meeting House Hill.

Distance 10 miles
Time 3½ hours

Cross to Norwich. Straight through village. Middle road straight ahead at fork, one-half mile beyond village to cross-roads one-half mile farther on. Here, go over Rowell and Bradley Hills to Meeting House Hill, or, take road around east of hill and first left to Meeting House Hill. Return down east of hill to road and south to fork, left and first right. Straight to River Road and Norwich Station.

11. Fay Hill and Allen Hill.

Distance 11 miles
Time 3½ hours

South on Lebanon Street, straight up hill at fork to State road, left towards Etna, first right across brook, by farm house up hill to notch. Across field on right to top of Fay Hill and on to Allen Hill. Down southeast side to road, taking right at fork to State road. Right at fork in State road and straight to Hanover; or, left at Fork to Lebanon, out Hanover Street and left at fork up hill to Hanover.

En tour over hills near Hanover

F. Harris '11.

How have the mighty fallen

12. HAPPY HILL.

Distance 11 miles
Time 4 hours

Same as No. 7 to Bragg Schoolhouse. Straight road (dotted on map) past schoolhouse, up brook to flat near the top. Wood road, or straight, through the brush, to the top, where an excellent view is obtained, both to the east and of the Green Mountains to the west. Return same way or via Dothan (No. 7).

13. HARTFORD.

Distance 12 miles
Time 3½ hours

Cross to Norwich Station. Left hand road over R.R. past mill and up hill. Straight to Hartford. Return by same way, by Wilder (No. 5), by White River Junction and Wilder (No. 8), or, by White River Junction and West Lebanon (No. 8).

14. ETNA AND HANOVER CENTER.

Distance 14 miles
Time 4 hours

South on Lebanon Street, straight up hill at fork to State Road. Left on State road to Etna. Straight about two miles to Hanover Center. From here Moose Mountain can be seen about a mile and a half to the east. Take first left about one-half mile beyond the church, then left by farm house at Spencer's Hill, where a fine view is obtained of the river to the north. Take dim road to right just before reaching the next farm house, down the stream to Lyme road at Gulick's farm.

15. LORD'S HILL.

Distance 14 miles
Time 4 hours

Balch Hill via Wheelock Street. Right at fork beyond top and straight at cross-roads. This leads into another road about one mile farther on and, going to the right here, turn back to the left about one-quarter mile beyond (road dotted on map). Across fields or right at farm house on "Wolfboro Road" to top of hill. Take trail to left along top of Lord's Hill, striking road at northern end. Left down valley to Lyme road and Hanover. From the top of the Hill an excellent view is obtained of Moose Mountain on the east and of the Green Mountains to the west. Some of the White Mountains can also be seen, especially from the northern end.

16. MOOSE MOUNTAIN CABIN.

(Red Trails "A" and "A 1".) Distance 16 miles
Time 5 hours

Follow No. 15 to the Wolfboro Road on top of Lord's Hill, or, No. 6 to cross-roads beyond Reservoir, thence straight to farm house at bottom of steep hill, taking dotted left hand road at fork up the hill, and straight at the farm house on the Wolfboro Road.

Down the east side of Lord's Hill to Hanover Center or follow the trail across the fields.   At Hanover Center take right beyond church and left at fork to top of hill then right to old Bradbury Farm.   Left across field opposite the house to trail and follow trail to cabin.   Return by same route or via Etna.

17.   MOOSE MOUNTAIN CABIN.   (Via ETNA.)

Distance 18 miles
Time   6 hours

Take No. 14 to Hanover Center and No. 16 to the Cabin. Return by same route, by No. 14, or No. 16.   Either of these

Madison Hut Trip. Mt. Adams in the distance

trips (No. 16 or No. 17) makes a delightful afternoon walk, taking supper at the Cabin and returning in the evening, or it is a very pleasant overnight trip as there are good accommodations, and the Cabin is free to any one desiring to go there.   Parties intending to spend a night there however, are requested to notify the Secretary of the Outing Club beforehand in order that there may be no conflicts.

18.   THETFORD AND LYME   Distance 20 miles
Time   an afternoon

Same as No. 8 to Pompanoosuc.   Straight to Thetford and across bridge to New Hampshire side.   State road to right, down river to Hanover.   This makes an ideal afternoon drive or sleigh ride or can be taken as a 10 mile walk up the river, taking supper at Thetford and returning on the evening train.

19. HOLT'S LEDGE.   Distance   (Train) 20 miles
                                                    (Foot) 11 miles
                         Time   One day; or,
                                     One afternoon

Take train from Norwich Station about 8 A.M. or 2 P.M. north to Thetford.   Cross river by bridge to Lyme, taking left at fork, about one-half mile from bridge.   Straight to Lyme Center and right about one-half mile beyond by farm house.   Follow this road to the farm on the hill, and there go straight across the field up the hill to the trail.   Follow this to near the top, then take left hand trail to the top of the Ledge.   This is a vertical cliff about 400 feet high and from the top a fine view is obtained. Return same way, taking train from Thetford about 1.30 P.M. or 7.30 P.M.

20. MT. CARDIGAN.   Distance   (Train) 50 miles
                                                    (Foot) 10 miles
                         Time   One day

Take train about 6 A.M. from Norwich Station south to Canaan, N. H.   Take straight road east through village and turn to right across brook just beyond.   Keep to right, along brook to Orange. Here take right across brook and left to trail up the Mountain. This makes a very delightful trip for one day, taking lunch along and eating on the top, then returning the same way to Canaan and taking the evening train about 6 P.M.   As no water can be obtained above the tree line, it must be carried up from a spring just below.   The view from the top of Cardigan is one of the best of any of the mountains near Hanover, and, as the climb is easy, this is a comfortable trip for ladies.

21. MT. ASCUTNEY.   Distance (Train) 38 miles
                                                  (Foot) 16 miles
                         Time   One day

Take south bound train about 6 A.M. to Windsor, Vt.   West through the town, past the jail, and take left-hand road along Mill Brook for about four miles.   Take left-hand road up hill after crossing the brook to the foot of Mt. Ascutney.   The path up the mountain turns off across the fields to left by farm house. From here it is about three miles to the top of the mountain and is very steep most of the way, but the path is good and it makes a delightful climb.   There is a fine spring about half way up and another about 200 yards west of the cabin down over the rocks, and the cabin affords very good shelter for any who desire to spend the night on the top and get the beautiful view of the sunrise for which Ascutney is famous.

The return is made by the same route to Windsor, where the evening train is taken for Hanover about 7 P.M.

22.   MT. CUBA.   Distance (Train) 36 miles
                                        (Foot) 16 miles
                            Time   One day

Take north bound train about 8 A.M. to Fairlee, Vt.   Cross to Orford, N. H., straight to Orfordville (3 miles), take middle road here for Cuba, past Morrison Stock Farm, taking left at fork, to Mt. Cuba House on shoulder of the mountain.   Across fields opposite the house to upper right hand corner of pasture, where the wood road leads up to the path.   A fine spring is found a little way up the path and good water is usually found nearly to the top.   The return is made by the same way and can be done in time to take the evening train to Hanover about 7 P.M.   If so desired, a team can be procured in Fairlee very cheaply, and it is easy to drive as far as the Mt. Cuba House, which is within a mile and a half of the top.

23.   MT. MOOSILAUKE. Distance via Glencliff
                                    (Train) 39 miles
                                    (Foot) 10 miles
                                 via Warren
                                    (Train) 44 miles
                                    (Foot) 20 miles
                          Time   One day, or One day
                                    and one night

Take train about 8 A.M. to Conicut, Vt.   Cross bridge to New Hampshire side and straight to Haverhill.   Left to church, then right to Haverhill station and take train south to Glencliff or Warren.

VIA GLENCLIFF.

Take road toward Sanitarium until within about one-quarter mile of it, where the path leads off across the fields to the right by an old barn.   This is hard to find at first and is very difficult to follow in places, so should not be attempted by any one who does not know it, except with a guide.   It is about five miles up this way, and the return can be made by the same path, but it is better to return by the carriage road to Warren.

VIA WARREN.

Take road to north from Warren station, then right, following the east branch of the stream, to Breezy Point.   Here take the carriage road to the summit, keeping to the right at fork in the woods.

Return either way, taking the evening train north to Haverhill and walking to Conicut in time to take the evening train from there down the river to Hanover. This trip can be taken in this way as a one day's trip, but it is advised to take the train up the afternoon before and spend the night at either Woodsville or Haverhill, taking the early morning train down to Glencliff. This gives more time and makes it a great deal more pleasant.

24. THE WHITE MOUNTAINS. (MT. WASHINGTON.)

Distance (Train) 180 miles
(Foot) Variable
Time Three days or more

Take the afternoon train north to Randolph, N. H., where the Ravine House makes a very good headquarters from which to make side trips, returning each night. The Glen House, at the foot of Mt. Washington and nine miles from Randolph, makes an ideal headquarters, but is not open during the winter. It is easy, however, to drive over from the Ravine House and start the trips from there, returning each night to the Ravine House. There are innumerable trips which can be taken, all of which are extremely beautiful and fascinating, but the most important are: —to the top of Mt. Washington; to Tuckerman's Ravine via the Raymond Path; to King's Ravine; to the Great Gulf; to the Madison Hut; to Wildcat; and to Mt. Adams.

There are also a great many others which can be taken and in the summer continuous trips can be made, with stops at a different place each night, but in the winter it is more advisable to keep some place as headquarters.

25. THE GREEN MOUNTAINS. (MT. MANSFIELD.)

Distance (Train) 96 miles
(Foot) Variable
Time Two days or more

Take Central Vermont R.R. from White River Junction to Waterbury, Vt., and from there take electrics to Stowe, Vt. From Waterbury a trail leads up Camel's Hump, which makes a very delightful day's climb, and from Stowe, Mt. Mansfield offers many opportunities.

There are also many other interesting trips in this vicinity which may be taken either in summer or in winter.

APPENDIX

DARTMOUTH OUTING CLUB

OFFICERS 1912-1913

C. E. Shumway . . .	*President*
M. C. Avery . . .	*Vice-President*
J. Y. Cheney . .	*Secretary*
D. E. Adams . . .	*Treasurer*
G. B. Watts . . .	*Fifth Member Executive Committee*

OFFICERS SEASON OF 1911-1912

W. Lee White . . .	*President*
A. T. Cobb	*Vice-President*
H. E. Allen	*Secretary*
M. C. Avery	*Treasurer*
C. E. Shumway . . .	*Executive Adviser*

OFFICERS SEASON OF 1910-1911

Fred H. Harris . . .	*President*
A. T. Cobb . . .	*Vice-President*
W. Lee White . . .	*Secretary*
W. H. Weston . . .	*Treasurer*
Prof. G. F. Hull,	
Prof. E. F. Clark	*Executive Advisers*

Constitution of the Dartmouth Outing Club

ARTICLE 1. NAME.

The name of this organization shall be:—The Dartmouth Outing Club.

ARTICLE 2. OBJECT.

The object shall be the promotion of interest in outdoor sports, especial emphasis being laid upon winter sports.

ARTICLE 3. OFFICERS.

The officers shall be a President, Vice-President, Secretary, Treasurer, and an Executive Committee of five, including officers.

ARTICLE 4. MEMBERSHIP.*

Resident graduate, undergraduates, and members of the Faculty are eligible to membership.

ARTICLE 5. MEETINGS.

Meetings shall be held at least monthly during the college year. Special meetings may be called by the President at any time.

ARTICLE 6. ELECTION OF OFFICERS.

Officers shall be elected by a majority vote at the last regular meeting of each college year.

ARTICLE 7. DUES.

The Treasurer shall collect a membership fee from all members, the amount of such fee to be determined by a majority of the members.

Rules for Perpetual Ski-Jumping Trophy

PRESENTED BY MR. C. A. HARRIS OF BRATTLEBORO, VT.

The Trophy shall be a championship honor to the ski-jumpers of the college, any undergraduate being eligible to compete annually.

A series of contests shall be held each winter for this purpose, the first jumper to win two of these contests being judged the winner of the Trophy for one year and shall have his name engraved on the cup together with the date.

The rules governing the contests for the Trophy shall be the same as those governing the Winter Carnival Senior Ski-jump, and this contest shall count as the first leg of the series for the Trophy.

*Proposed First Amendment.
ARTICLE 4 to read:—Dartmouth Alumni, graduate students, undergraduates and members of the Faculty are eligible to membership.

The Winter Carnival has been described elsewhere in this book.　Below are given the names of the winners of first and second prizes and the times or number of points made in all the different events.

1911

Event	Winner	Second	Time
Snowshoe Cross-Country	W. T. Jones '12	J. L. Day '14	25 min., 39¾ sec.
Ski Cross-Country	F. H. Harris '11	A. T. Cobb '12	25 min., 5½ sec.
Snowshoe Obstacle Race	T. P. Miller '12	H. E. Allen '12	
Ski 100 Yard Dash	A. T. Cobb '12	V. C. Schellenberg '13	18.4 sec.
Ski 220 Yard Dash	A. T. Cobb '12	C. E. Shumway '13	
Snowshoe 100 Yard Dash	J. L. Day '14	G. B. Watts '13	18 seconds
Snowshoe 220 Yard Dash	A. S. Holway '12	J. L. Day '14	38 seconds
Senior Ski-jump	A. T. Cobb '12 285 points	F. H. Harris '11 280 points	52 ft. 3 in.
Novice Ski-Jump	W. H. Weston '11	No second prize	
Junior Ski-Jump	John Bowler	No second prize	

1912

Event	Winner	Second	Time
Snowshoe Cross-country	J. L. Day '14	A. S. Holway '12	23 min., 29 secs.
Ski Cross-Country	A. T. Cobb '12	J. Bache-Wiig '15	23 min. 56 secs.
Snowshoe Obstacle Race	D. E. Adams '13	W. L. Baldwin '13	
Ski 100 Yard Dash	A. T. Cobb '12	J. Bache-Wiig '15	22⅖ seconds
Ski 220 Yard Dash	J. Y. Cheney '13	J. Bache-Wiig '15	
Snowshoe 100 Yard Dash	M. Haskell '14	A. S. Holway '12	18¼ seconds
Snowshoe 220 Yard Dash	J. L. Day '14	A. S. Holway '12	39¼ seconds
Senior Ski-jump	A. T. Cobb '12 * (281 Points)	D. T. Rogers '15 (280 Points)	47¼ feet
Novice Ski-jump	G. F. Fox '13	J. Bache-Wiig '15	
Junior Ski-jump	B. J. Dinwald	John Densmore	

*First place was won by F. H. Harris '11, with a total of 306 points to Cobb's 281 points, but being an alumnus, he could not compete for the prize.

Carnival Scene, 1911

CPSIA information can be obtained at www.ICGtesting.com
Printed in the USA
BVOW04s2229300414

352236BV00010B/128/P

9 781166 589196